Why

Women

The Leadership Imperative to Advancing Women and Engaging Men

Jeffery Tobias Halter

Why Women
The Leadership Imperative to Advancing Women and Engaging Men
Copyright© 2015 Jeffery Tobias Halter.

Published By:
Fushian LLC, d/b/a YWomen
320 Thorndale Court
Roswell, GA 30075
www.ywomen.biz

Jeffery Tobias Halter
http://ywomen.biz/

Author: Jeffery Tobias Halter
Book layout and design: Steven Sharp
Book cover design: Jeffery Tobias Halter
Photo: Andrew Wehrenberg
Copy editing: Betsy Rhame-Minor
Editor: John Fayad
Seventh Printing: September 2016

ISBN: 978-0-9861425-0-5
1. Business
Manufactured in the United States of America
Printed in the United States of America by:
BookLogix, Alpharetta, GA

This paper meets the requirements of ANSI/NISO Z39.48-1992
(Permanence of Paper)

Dedication

This book is dedicated to my wife and best friend, Phyllis
and our children,
Heather and George, Jeff Jr. and Lauren.

This book is also dedicated to fathers of daughters who realize the
incredible responsibility they have for supporting the advancement of
women in the workplace and in the world.

Table of Contents

Foreword

I had the pleasure of meeting Jeffery Tobias Halter for the first time in the fall of 2013. As founder of the Center for Women in Business at Bentley University, I was helping to conduct a symposium on Engaging Men to Advance Women in Business. Jeffery was our closing keynote speaker and it was the first time I was introduced to his YWomen's Integrated Women's Leadership framework.

In Jeffery's words, "We don't need to convince women about the need for change, we need to convince men. Men still occupy almost 85 percent of the executive positions in corporate America. If we are to drive long-term systemic change in organizations we must have ownership from the highest level of the organization, and today that is still men."

Engaging men is truly the new frontier for advancing the women's leadership agenda. How can it be that women hold just 10 to 15 percent of the senior leadership positions in corporate America? Why haven't we made more progress given that women represent 58 percent of our college graduates and hold 50 percent of middle management positions, with 40 percent holding positions that include purchasing authority? The statistics go on and on and numbers alone are not enough to convince male leaders to change.

Yes, of course, there has been progress along the way; and yes today we have more female leaders than a generation ago, but the numbers are still very small at the top organizations. To make matters worse, the conversations we're having about gender and work today are the very same conversations we were having when I was President Clinton's advisor on women's issues in the White House during the mid-1990s. It seems like yesterday, but we've been at this for almost twenty-five years. I'm not talking about the post-60s feminist movement, but the true business integration of talented women that began in the early 90s. While it is positive to reflect on the now over twenty female CEOs in corporate America, it is a sad statement to make that out of the Fortune 500, approximately 475 are led by men.

We reach for programs and initiatives that might help us, and some such as sponsorship, flexibility and accountability—are moving the needle. But corporate leaders and their teams are frustrated by the lack of gender progress as well as the gender tension (both overt and covert) that still permeates organizations. In an age of political correctness, men and women are forced to hide their true selves at work for fear of saying or doing the wrong thing. All of this strains energy and emotion, and even worse, engagement and productivity for companies.

The good news is that many companies are in fact reaching consensus on the need to advance women. Many CEOs are no longer asking "why" they should include advancing women in their organizations but "how" to begin to do it.

Why Women, the Leadership Imperative to Advancing Women and Engaging Men is written to tackle this question of how to build an end-to-end corporate solution. As Jeffery points out "the problem is, companies have intellectualized the numbers and the objectives, but they've never internalized it, placed economic value on it, and held their organizations responsible for truly driving change." Too often today in organizations, what passes for gender efforts, is a series of discussions, and disjointed programs and processes in which women find themselves talking to other women. I know from my own experience that my goal was often merely to get budget, signoff, and resources from leadership to move my agenda on women forward within the organization. For many of us in this field, this is been a meaningful and productive strategy, but it hasn't been woven into the fabric of the organization. And, in many occasions, a committed CEO, with the best of intentions, has gone away believing that his support, plus periodic face time was sufficient.

What we know for sure is that what got us here won't get us there. Companies need to acknowledge that what they are doing is simply not working. It is not moving the needle and it is not preparing their organizations for a future workforce that is increasingly female and multicultural. The old saying is true; insanity is doing the same things and expecting different results. But to get to a different result – to truly support, retain and promote women in the workplace and capitalize on women in the marketplace—shouldn't we be engaging men in the conversation as full partners?

Why Women, the Leadership Imperative to Advancing Women and Engaging Men is a business book written by a business leader. In business language, Jeffery articulates the three simple reasons for corporations to think strategically about women: 1) to grow revenue, 2) to improve operating profit, and 3) to enhance company reputation. Jeffery examines the critical need to engage every function within the organization in the strategy ultimately resulting in scorecarding and hard metrics. Most importantly, we must do so with a sense of urgency as the world we compete in today is changing in an ever-escalating manner. This is a must-read guide for all leaders in an organization, not just women or HR professionals but for men and line leaders who want to know how to win with women today.

Jeffery is a passionate advocate for the advancement of women and his stories provide insights into his own epiphany regarding the power of women in organizations. And while the book is filled with research and data, he knows that all the data in the world will not move men from passive participants to active champions.

To move men to advocacy it takes a personal connection and in Jeffery's case it is being the father of a daughter. Jeffery believes that fathers of daughters have an absolute responsibility to be advocates in the workplace. To quote from the book, "As a business leader I need to realize that if I am not advocating for women in my workplace today then no one is going to advocate for my daughter ten years from now when she's faced with the same biases, challenges, inequities and, quite frankly, bullshit, that I see women put up with today. As the father of a daughter this is just unacceptable."

Engaging men in the advancement of women is truly the new frontier for every company in America, and this is the book that will show you how to do it.

Betsy Myers is the Founding Director of the Center for Women in Business at Bentley University. Betsy is the former COO and Chair of Women for President Obama's 2008 national presidential campaign, and during the Clinton administration she was the first director of the White House Office for Women's Initiatives and Outreach. Betsy is also the author of the best-selling business book, Take the Lead.

Chapter 1

The Epiphany!

"We must therefore strive to achieve nothing less than total enterprise realignment around this awesome, burgeoning, astoundingly untapped market!"

—Tom Peters,
Re-imagine! Business Excellence in a Disruptive Age [1]

"I'm a straight white guy. What the heck do I know about Diversity?" Those were my first thoughts almost 15 years ago. The Coca-Cola Company had just settled a $200 million discrimination lawsuit and I was being asked to lead an initiative on diversity education. My background was as a sales manager and a business leader. What did I do wrong to get this assignment?

This was an event that would change my life and be the start of my epiphany regarding women in leadership.

Like most male leaders, I didn't know what I didn't know. Not just about this "women's" thing, but about all the things that we as male leaders pay no attention to on a daily basis—such as sexism, bias, and "white male privilege." These are the things I would learn deep lessons around in the ensuing years. Now, before you begin to think that this is just another one of those touchy-feely diversity books stuck on the worn out arguments of compliance and fairness, let me set the record straight and, for once, move this dialog forward:

I AM A RAVING CAPITALIST!

I want you to read this book and make more money—for yourself and your organization! If you ask most senior business leader today, one simple question, "What keeps you up at night?" I guarantee, you will hear one or more of at least three major issues:

Major Challenges Facing CEOs [2]

1. Customer relations/growing revenue
2. Human capital/growing people
3. Operational excellence/growing operating profit

Business today is tough. Every organization is faced with their share of the same financial challenges and constraints. Since 2008, companies have met many organizational goals with mid to flat revenue growth. While this strategy was accepted at the time and necessary for economic recovery, shareholders are now demanding a return to growth strategies. Wall Street analysts are challenging companies saying, "You can no longer cut and save your way to earnings results, we need to see revenue growth." [3]

"I need to drive topline growth in these challenging times."

Similarly, pressure is still on to continue to drive ever-increasing operating profits. Since 2008, organizations have worked diligently to cut costs, expenses, and people. The challenge now is to accelerate growth rates of operating profits to the high, single-digit to double-digit rates that had been achieved through cost-cutting and improved efficiency. The fat was cut a long time ago and we are well into the bone. We must now find new ways to drive efficiency.

"We must re-examine every aspect of our business that is not maximizing operating profit."

The final thing keeping leaders up at night is something that is rarely talked about but always in the front of their mind. There has never been a time where more focus has been paid to company reputation than in today's business and social environment. In this day and age of corporate hackers, websites, and social media channels, everyone is aware of what goes on in a company. Companies today are constantly being questioned and criticized in social media at every turn. Being a good corporate citizen is no longer enough. You need to manage your company reputation proactively, aggressively, and on a daily basis.

"My company's reputation is always on the line now, and under constant scrutiny."

These three issues are the number one reason for companies to rethink their points of view on women. Women today are one of the most significant untapped and underutilized resources in your company.

The purpose of this book is very straightforward. I want you to embrace an integrated organizational approach to women in your organization. Not because it is a nice thing to do but because it is an absolute business imperative. There are three very simple reasons you must treat this as a business imperative.

> *Growing revenue, improving operating profits, and enhancing your company reputation are the three primary reasons to implement an Integrated Women's Leadership Strategy.*

At this point, you may be asking yourself, why is a man writing a book about realigning the entire organization around this opportunity called women? Well, I gave you part of the reason. I am a capitalist . . . and a business consultant. Through an extraordinary set of circumstances, I have spent a significant portion of the last fifteen years focused on women, business, and leadership.

In his book, *The Outliers: The Story of Success,* [4] Malcolm Gladwell defines an expert as someone who has put in a minimum of 10,000 hours of study on a given subject. By that definition, and compared to most men, I am an expert in the field of women in business and organizations.

However, when my expertise is compared to the average woman, I unabashedly admit that I don't have a clue as to her motivations, challenges, struggles, and the issues that she deals with on an hourly and daily basis. But I am aware, deeply engaged in the conversation, and taking action. It has taken me over thirty years to figure this out and frankly, we don't have time to wait any longer.

The purpose of this book is to create powerful conversations in organizations to drive business results with a sense of urgency. This book is written for senior leaders in organizations, both men and women. That being said, my belief is the primary purchasers of this book will be senior women and HR professionals. As you will see throughout the book, most men and most organizations are not ready to have this conversation. My goal is to change organizational conversations regarding women and to support, educate, and embrace advocates for change.

As one of the female participants in a focus group pointed out upon reading my draft manuscript,

I immediately wanted to give a copy to every male colleague and say "Read this book!"

One of the most powerful lessons I learned in working with women is that you really don't have to convince them that this is a good idea. They already get it. They live with issues and challenges every day. My job is to convince men (and quite frankly, a few women) that this is really a good thing for them and their organization.

Men also need to hear this message from another man. They need to hear it from a guy who's been on the front line with bottom line responsibility—and has the scars to prove it. I am going to provide you with facts and data. I'm a man, and if you're going to convince other men you will need facts and data. Additionally I will say that many men and many organizations are starting to realize the importance of women to their organizations and to their bottom line.

The primary issue that's lacking in most organizations is a true sense of urgency.

It's very easy for leaders to intellectualize these concepts, but it takes an entirely different mindset to internalize them and take action, and do so with a sense of urgency.

We have been talking about women in the workplace and marketplace for over twenty years but the pace of change lacks a true sense of urgency. That should be the goal for leadership and it is the goal of this book.

As a man, it is also not my intent to throw men under the bus. This is not a male-bashing, hyper-feminist left-wing conspiracy book. This book is plainly written for business and executive leaders (still 84 percent men) who want to solve their biggest business issues.

I believe that women provide one of the best solutions for doing this, yet men have a difficult time adjusting to this new line of sight. Men tend to function very well and are quite comfortable in today's world of business and it's not hard to understand why. The world of business was designed by men for men at a time when companies were populated almost exclusively by men. For that underlying reason, it's difficult for men to view their workplace from any other perspective.

Nevertheless, as a leader, you need to take a hard look around the table at your organization and form a realistic view. Chances are, your organization and your leadership team are comprised of people who will never comprehend, let alone be able to internalize and operationalize, these concepts. Increasingly, more men in positions of leadership are questioning the past and developing this new line of sight.

"I don't think we have any"

The best example of a company having its own epiphany is one I had the privilege to work with a few years ago. It is a mid-sized publicly traded company with a great corporate culture, great growth, and terrific profits. It is a proto-typical great place to work. Yet, when the company president looked around the table at his executive team, he saw eight white men looking back at him and he said,

> ***"Gentlemen, I don't know much about this 'Diversity Thing,' but as I look around me, I don't think we have any."***

When you look at your leadership team, what does it look like? Chances are it looks just like this president's team. What's important to note is that they were already very successful. It would have been easy to maintain status quo. Instead this visionary leader realized they were missing something. That's how simple this is . . . and how hard.

Now I know what many of the men are thinking right now: "Eight white men at a table can in fact be diverse." I will acknowledge that this is true and I would never seek to homogenize any group of individuals. That being said, chances are, most of these men act, behave, and think in a manner very similar to the other men sitting at the table. These men arrived at their position in the company by performing and acting in a very similar manner to the seven other white men in the room.

As I said they were successful but yet realized they were missing something because . . .

> **If you look, think and act like me . . .**
> **why do I need you at this table?**

More importantly, do you think, act, and represent the mindset of the majority of your employees and customers? These are important foundational thoughts, but here is how I will break it all down and operationalize the approach for you.

WHY WOMEN

Part One of our book examines how, as leaders of the organization, you need to **Internalize** the business case for women. Part Two draws attention to the five critical business functions needed to **Operationalize** a women's strategy. And Part Three is when everything comes together to guide and **Transform** your organization to a position of strength and success.

Part One will focus on the failure of organizations to truly think of women in a strategic way. Why? Because the strategic business case hasn't been made strongly and crisply enough by leaders who have real bottom line responsibility. The real value is beyond compelling.

The problem is . . .

Leadership has intellectualized the numbers and the objectives, but they've never internalized it, placed economic value on it, and held their organizations responsible for truly driving change.

Most organizations have failed to think strategically about women as a business opportunity and the potential solution to their biggest business problems. In Part One, we will set the context for creating a Strategic Integrated Women's Leadership Framework. We will examine why it's hard to do and examine what a solid foundation looks like.

What Men Aren't Telling Women

Chapter 2 is written for raging capitalists and for the women who want to know what men think about this topic. The answers may surprise you.

I will share the three things that you will NEVER hear a man say regarding women in organizations.

We will take a very practical approach and examine the primary reasons to launch a total enterprise realignment for women. And we will explore why change has been so slow in coming.

The 80/80/80 Solution

Chapter 3 will provide a specific measureable business case for change, which I term "The 80/80/80 Solution." The numbers you will examine are your company's numbers, so you really won't be able to debate them. These numbers will motivate you to take a critical look at why we should even bother doing this work.

Having established the "Why" of the business case, we will then begin to look at the "How." How do you begin to operationalize your plan through your existing business functions, processes, and systems?

Part Two of the book will examine the critical business functions that are the most important for success. Specifically, I will take a deep dive into the responsibilities and interdependencies of:

- Marketing and Sales
- Operations and the Field
- Human Resources
- Senior Management
- Corporate Communications and Company Reputation

The $20 Trillion "Niche"

Globally, women spend $20 trillion annually, yet many companies still consider women a specialty market segment instead of the dominant force they are. In the United States, that number is $7 trillion. Chapter 4 will focus on sales and marketing and the machine known as the "American Female Shopper." Women in the United States today spend more money than the economies of India and China combined! [5] And while this should be a convincing statistic for business leaders interested in who's driving the U.S. economy . . .

Many organizations still view the female shopper as a niche!

In our chapter, "The $20 Trillion Niche," we will not only look at the market opportunity, but we will examine the challenges and issues many organizations and industries' marketing and sales functions are facing in trying to do this right.

The Field Factor

Chapter 5 uncovers probably the greatest challenge facing organizations today. It is also the least talked about, researched, and understood. We will take a deep dive into that corporate area called "The Field." This is where CEOs come from and it is a virtual desert for women to navigate. The C-suite is populated by line managers and leaders—those with sales, operating, and supply chain roles, and those with P&L responsibilities. I will show you that almost . . .

Every one of the female CEOs in America today has come from or spent time in the field.

In "The Field Factor" we will examine how meritocracies really play themselves out and how the nature of the work, organizational requirements, and personal challenges combine to create a "perfect storm" of issues that prohibit women from staying and advancing to the highest level of the organization.

The HR Paradox

Chapter 6 focuses on human capital and the programs and processes of Human Resources. In "The HR Paradox," we will examine the critical programs that are necessary in recruiting, retaining, and advancing women and why HR alone cannot be the sole owner of this responsibility.

There has never been a greater time in business history for Human Resources to redefine their role as strategists and secure a more important seat at the table.

I will examine critical and interdependent HR programs and processes that are not only important to winning with women but also necessary for winning with all employees.

The Leadership Imperative

Chapter 7 focuses the critical role of leadership today to creating an Integrated Women's Leadership Strategy that holds the organization accountable. Today, companies measure every aspect of their business—from production, to sales, to profit—and they hold people accountable for quality, goal attainment, and efficiency. Yet in most companies, the critical and future-defining element of "women's leadership" is missing in that set of critical metrics. In many organizations, it's not even acknowledged.

This chapter will examine how organizations can create a true Integrated Women's Leadership Scorecard and hold people accountable for their relevant deliverables and success. We will also examine the role of Senior Leadership—not just HR—in owning a "Leadership Mindset" around the Scorecard.

The Company Reputation Connection

Chapter 8 examines the final, but perhaps most overlooked element in a strategic plan: the role of company reputation. This last critical element serves as both one of the reasons "to do this" and also is one of the Key Business Levers. Your Company Reputation is an expectation and if you are a publicly traded company today, the public and your shareowners are looking to you for leadership.

The timing and importance of this function have never been more important and I will examine the connection that women can play in supporting, or jeopardizing, your brands, your workplace, and your overall company reputation.

In Part Three, "Realigning the Organization for Success," I will provide an Organizational Toolkit that focuses on the critical factors needed to make this all work including, middle manager buy-in, male engagement, and other issues we never talk about in the hallways of corporate America.

The Need for Male Champions

Chapter 9 discusses one of the most significant keys to operationalizing your women's strategy. Engaging men as champions and visual advocates who recognize the value of women is the cornerstone of organizational success. I believe that upwards of 20 percent of men are "ready-now" and willing to support the advancement of women. The actual number may even be higher. Men just need to be invited into the conversation.

I will explore the characteristics of Male Champions and why this is such a tough topic for men. We will look at how most of a man's upbringing and cultural male norms work against us to support women in the workplace. Finally,

> *I will discuss the absolute responsibility*
> *that I believe fathers of daughters have to*
> *becoming visible and vocal advocates for women.*

The Unmentionables

Chapter 10 will examine a few of the things that are rarely talked about in workplace settings. What are the real and often hidden impediments that most organizations face in executing an Integrated Women's Leadership Strategy? I'll examine organizational barriers and how companies can overcome them. I'll also explore personal challenges that often arise and have the potential to thwart your efforts in doing this work effectively.

The RAVING CAPITALIST Action Plan

My summary at the end of the book will provide the actions needed to attack this work with a sense of urgency. This will provide you a final checklist to finalize your leadership strategy. This will not only serve as a recap for the plan you've written with me throughout this book, but also offer a summary checklist of the most important elements to winning with women. Finally, I will provide a glimpse into future trends that will be impacting the future of women, men, and organizations in the next five years . . . and beyond.

I began this introductory chapter by declaring that women can be the solution to some of your organization's biggest problems such as growing topline revenue, driving increased operating profit, and enhancing your company reputation.

Women are in the news every day, from powerful statistics on their influence in the marketplace, to cable news and talk shows on leadership, to global summits on women's rights and values. This topic is only going to become more important.

As a leader, you have two choices: you can choose to ignore this obvious opportunity or you can harness it to improve the bottom line results of your organization.

You will notice the word "YWomen" used multiple times in my book. YWomen, is the name of my strategic consulting practice. The "Y" represents the Y chromosome, which as you know is the biological differentiator between a male and a female. My work focuses on creating integrated women's leadership strategies by engaging men (i.e., the Y chromosomes). This is accomplished by engaging both men and women in a meaningful business dialogue regarding the power of women in organizations.

YWomen is designed to serve as a constant reminder to the reader that this work cannot be successful without engaging men in women's leadership initiatives.

It's 2015. Why are we still talking about Women and Diversity?

Many millennials, both young men and women, question why we are still talking about this topic. Haven't we moved past this? Progressive companies like Tom's Shoes, Zappos, and Whole Foods aren't even talking about gender. Isn't great leadership genderless? The short answer is yes. The longer answer is many companies still haven't figured this out. Whether it is corporate culture, historical barriers, or a host of other organizational issues many companies are acknowledging they have challenges and what they have done in the past isn't working.

For this reason you will note that I often will use the words "women" and "diversity" interchangeably. While my work today focuses primarily on women, the frameworks, question raised, and the solutions are also applicable to many of today's organizational issues regarding race, multiculturalism, age, sexual orientation, and other deeper dimensions of diversity. My belief is, if organizations cannot have meaningful and actionable conversations regarding women then it may be premature to have a deeper dialogue regarding other types of differences in the marketplace and workplace.

How to Read this Book

First, every chapter starts out with a story. Stories are one of the critical ways to deepen your cultural competency in an area. These personal stories are designed to guide you to your own epiphany as they have for me. Each is true and each is served as a key learning moment in my journey. My hope is these stories will speed your learnings as you do not have time to waste to have your epiphany.

Second, look for the,

Call-outs that appear mid-page in bold. These are key quotes to help you quickly glean an idea. Many have a footnote which you can examine in greater detail in the reference list.

Third, as you as read you will find bullets in boxes.

> **W** These are significant facts, data, and research that can provide provocative discussion topics for your organization.

Fourth, at the end of each chapter, you will find **Summary Points** of the key concepts from the chapter. The summary points are also ideal as ready-made discussion points for meetings with individuals, teams, or larger operating units in the organization.

Fifth, at the end of each chapter are a series of **WHY WOMEN Readiness Assessment** questions. These questions will be asked at the end of each chapter and also summarized at the end of the book to form a thirty-point organizational readiness assessment.

Finally, I will reference **Deepening Your Learning** elements. These are various books, links, and case studies that you can examine to deepen your learning in these areas.

Why Women: The Leadership Imperative to Advancing Women and Engaging Men, is 100 percent dependent on you taking action, questioning the status quo, and examining this opportunity with the sense of urgency you would give to any other $100 million new project.

Every year I attend a large number of women's leadership conferences and each event is invariably a sellout with standing room only crowds. Women today are hungry to learn, to lead, and to aspire to the highest ranks of every organization. There is a collectiveness growing in this country regarding women, and a tsunami of change on the horizon.

At these conferences, I am usually one of only a dozen men in attendance. I will tell you firsthand, you cannot stand in a room of 2,500 women without feeling the kinetic energy of their unity and optimism. The takeaway for me is clear,

The tsunami of change on the horizon is coming and it's called Women!

Summary Points from Chapter 1

- Most organizations have failed to think strategically about women as a business opportunity and how that strategy may possibly be the solution to some of their biggest business problems.

- For over twenty years, the business case has been clearly documented for women yet very little progress has been made. It simply hasn't been given a sense of urgency and articulated strongly enough by leaders with real bottom line responsibility.

- To be successful today, each sector of the organization must own a portion of your Women's Leadership Strategy and all sectors must be integrated in their business plan, metrics, policies, and procedures—including marketing, sales, operations, HR, and your senior leadership team.

- Your company reputation is under attack daily. Companies can no longer feel isolated and must work diligently to protect this valuable asset.

- Engaging men as champions and visual advocates who recognize the value of women is the cornerstone of organizational success. They must be leaders who get it and walk the talk every day in their actions and communications.

WHY WOMEN Readiness Assessment

1. If you think about the biggest issues that your organization is facing, those challenges that "keep you up at night," how can you better leverage an Integrated Women's Leadership Strategy as a potential solution?

2. As you look at the leadership team around you, does this group think, act, and truly represent the mindset of the majority of your employees and customers?

3. How is your organization moving from a conceptual conversation regarding women to strategies and programs that help to internalize and operationalize a women's leadership strategy for all employees?

Deepening Your Learning

— Book —

Reimagine!: Business Excellence in a Disruptive Age, Tom Peters

— Online Article —

"Can Women Fix Capitalism?" McKinsey & Company (Sep 2014)

— Website —

http://www.womenetics.com

Part 1:

The Failure to Internalize the Business Case

Chapter 2

What Men Aren't Telling Women

"We've seen what can be accomplished when we use 50 percent of our human capacity. If you visualize what 100 percent can do, you'll join me as an unbridled optimist about America's future."

—Warren Buffet, on underutilizing the talents of women [6]

I was invited to speak to the executive women of the Goizueta business school at Emory University in Atlanta, Georgia. They wanted to know how men feel and what men are talking about when it comes to women in business. The women attending wanted to know both the formal and informal. They wanted to know what men discuss in the boardroom and in the locker room. They wanted a peek under the tent into the world of men.

These women knew of my work in women's leadership and they knew that I would give them an honest answer. After interviewing a host of my male colleagues prior to the event, the answer became very simple but quite surprising for many of the women there.

The Three Things Men Aren't Telling Women

1. I don't understand why things need to change. What's different today that should cause me focus on women?

2. Even if I acknowledge why things needed to change, I don't know exactly what to change or how to change them.

3. To tell you the truth, I personally really don't care.

These were some of the most honest and direct reactions I had ever received! And as I thought back, I realized that the majority of the men I engage with in business every day have never really shared these innermost thoughts with me, let alone with their women colleagues.

Before I go any further, let me state that I DO know men who understand and value the contribution that women make. I know organizations with cultures that recognize and value the unique contribution of women. I know business leaders who understand the business case, and I know HR professionals who are aware of what needs to change, why, and how to support the organization in sustaining that change.

Nevertheless, the realization for me that day was that the majority of the men (and some of the women) had never even considered engaging women with a truly integrated, bottom-line value mindset. Three tenets emerged for me that day and became the focus of my talk, and ultimately the foundation for this book:

> **W** The *why* things need to change;
>
> **W** The *what* that has to change; and
>
> **W** The *who* that will drive change.

As I prepared my remarks and during my talk, I wasn't disheartened, but challenged in finding a way to increase the number of leaders who do understand and invite women into the conversation. The real question is, "Why is this so hard?" It's a question that almost answers itself when you scan our current business environment. The challenge for organizations is that they have not approached women as an "operating priority."

Most companies have never put an economic value on women's leadership.

If women were a true operating priority, organizations would have programs, budgets, processes, and metrics well in place—and they would hold people accountable with a demonstrated sense of urgency. Most importantly, as with all other operating priorities, organizations would have already done the hard work of determining what and where the opportunity gap is and how it can be closed—in this instance, by women. As I stated in Chapter 1, the three primary business reasons to create an Integrated Women's Leadership Strategy are to grow revenue, improve operating profit, and enhance company reputation.

The YWOMEN Integrated Women's Leadership Framework

To help illustrate this and bring visual context to the topic, we will create a strategic framework for your company. I will begin by using a standard business strategy quadrant analysis. I will illustrate revenue on a vertical axis (*growth*) and operating profit (*cost savings*) on a horizontal axis. Finally, as company reputation is driven by both revenue and operating profit, we will demonstrate this as a third axis.

YWomen Integrated Women's Leadership Framework

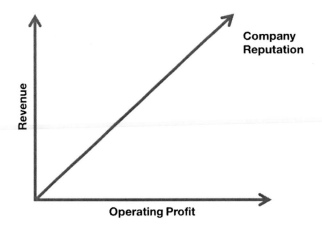

Revenue

Each year, companies commit weeks and months to developing the business and marketing plans that will deliver the results.

At the end of the day, there are only three ways to grow revenue:

1. Sell more of your exisitng products to customers, either by taking it out of your competitor's marketshare or through your customers' natural growth trends.

2. Prospect and acquire new customers for your company's goods and services.

3. Introduce a new product line or line extension of an existing product.

Each of these takes a significant amount of planning, running of growth scenarios, and understanding customer needs and trends—all to generate incremental models of growth.

The question is, have you taken a true look at women as a new source of revenue? This is not just a marketing exercise to see if we need a line extension or another campaign, but has the entire organization truly done the hard work to determine the size of the opportunity?

Does your organization see women as an opportunity and can they articulate in revenue dollars what the value of that growth is?

This framework is a good illustration of the challenging work organizations face in attempting to internalize the business case for women. The hard work is up front and includes conducting a thorough opportunity assessment of how much growth is actually available in the marketplace. Most of the organizations I work with cannot articulate in specific terms the revenue opportunity with women because they may not even see it. I will take a deeper dive into revenue drivers in our next chapter but for now let's examine just one example.

Defining your Revenue Gap

To demonstrate how your organization can benefit by thinking differently about this opportunity with women, let's explore one possible aspect of revenue growth: the opportunity to obtain new clients.

According to the *2014 State of Women-Owned Businesses Report* commissioned by American Express . . .

> **W**   Women today are starting 1,288 new businesses every day. This is double the rate from only three years ago. [7]

Their report, sourced from the U.S. Census Bureau, finds that over the past seventeen years the number of women-owned businesses grew at a rate **150 percent** of the national average.

As women's daily business creation hit a record pace, the number of women-owned firms reached a new milestone in 2014. The report estimates that there are more than 9.1 million women-owned businesses in the United States (compared to 8.6 million in 2013). These businesses generate more than $1.4 trillion in revenues, employ an additional 7.9 million people, and account for 30 percent of all enterprises. [8]

During the past seventeen years, women-owned businesses have steadily increased their influence on the U.S. economy. Since 1997 women-owned firms have:

> **W** Increased in number by 68 percent
>
> **W** Grown revenues by 72 percent
>
> **W** Added 11 percent more jobs to the U.S. economy

Nine million new small, women-owned businesses generating over $1.4 trillion in revenue is a watershed of potential new clients for companies.

As leaders, how are you challenging your organization to think differently about women as shoppers, consumers, and business owners? What is one possible new channel of revenue that could be unleased through a better understanding of the women's market?

Operating Profit

From a business planning approach, operating profit is often both a top-down and bottom-up process. Senior leadership examines the need for earning results, long-term infrastructure needs, and other significant capital projects. This includes the need for the cash flow necessary to position the organization for the future. At the same time, operating units are building customer plans and looking at a host of expenses to come up with those plans. For many companies, one of the most significant expense items is its people.

Since the economic collapse of 2008, most organizations have undergone major restructuring to trim back employee-associated costs. Layers of middle management have been stripped away, and many functions that were previously handled internally have been outsourced to other companies and countries.

After reductions in force and outsourcing, organizations are left with just a handful of drivers that are within a manager or leader's control. One of these is talent (the people that you recruit, retain, and develop) and the other is engagement.

Since 2008, companies have made very hard choices regarding people. However, in doing so, hard lessons have been learned about the true cost of talent. Though operating profit may capture the immediate gains from reductions in salary and benefits, it doesn't necessarily take into account the profitability/revenue generated on a per employee basis or the replacement cost of employees. Other costs include loss of efficiency, loss of organizational knowledge, and loss of future promotable talent. For now I will illustrate it as a driver of operating profit. Talent is one driver of revenue and profit, and the other is that of engagement and its impact on operating profit.

Today, organizations are beginning to realize that engagement is not merely a metric of employee satisfaction but the key to productivity, some believe more valuable than IQ, pedigree, or experience.

Engagement means Productivity

Each year, billions of dollars are spent building, assessing, and calibrating assembly line and machine processes with the goal of reaching and sustaining operating efficiencies of 100 percent. If I'm a production supervisor and I have a line that is running at 80 percent efficiency, I'm doing everything in my power to tweak a belt or twist a knob that will help drive that efficiency to 100 percent. Organizations need to prioritize employee productivity in the same manner as a true business metric and remove impediments and barriers to improve efficiency.

Today high performing companies strive for an engagement level of 80 percent. This means in even high-performing companies I am paying an employee for eight hours of work per day, and I am getting at best 6.4 good hours of work out of you.

> *The challenge is that the engagement level of many employees is far less than 50 percent. This means that, at best, I'm only getting four productive hours of work out of my employees in an eight hour day.* [9]

If you were a production line and I was only getting 50 percent productivity out of you in an eight-hour day, I would have engineers on the case figuring out what was wrong. Unfortunately, we don't take the same approach with our people—to understand if they're truly engaged and to troubleshoot any impediments that may be in their way and find the means for them to function at peak performance. These two topics of talent and engagement will be given specific business case metrics in our next chapter, The 80/80/80 Solution.

Company Reputation

Company reputation has sprinted its way up the list of critical metrics that need to be constantly monitored and calibrated. In today's world of twenty-four hour social media, customers, consumers, advocacy groups, and activists are all talking, tweeting, and blogging about your organization. We love to joke that if it appears on the Internet it must be true. Sadly, that is often the case for many organizations. Perception becomes reality if not managed.

The speed of communication by consumers, activists, and the investment community is exponentially faster than an organization's ability to respond.

Your company and its reputation must be high on your list of importance, because your employees will either support and enrich your reputation, or serve to tear it down. Environmental sustainability, corporate social responsibility, philanthropy, community involvement, and supplier diversity are all significant initiatives in which companies are investing to build stakeholder equity.

In the Context of Gender

There are many elements that comprise an organization's reputation—from compliance to community involvement, to carbon footprint. Organizations need to realize that women, more so than men, are more attentive to an organization's reputation. It's a critical value point to them and they're voting every day with their feet and their wallets.

We will explore each of these areas and their impact on the bottom line in Chapter 8, The Company's Reputation Connection.

A Strategic Framework Emerges

To summarize our framework, we have looked at the three business reasons as the impetus for beginning this work of women in leadership. We've also examined key elements underneath each one, and they are now represented on the framework below:

YWomen Integrated Women's Leadership Framework

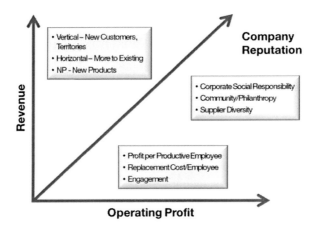

This framework allows us to begin to answer the first question raised by male leaders at the beginning of the chapter, "The why things need to change." The answer as I have previously stated is simple: to grow revenue, to improve operating profit, and to enhance company reputation. By visualizing a strategic framework we can now begin to align all organizational functions into an efficient operating model and also put into place metrics and accountability.

Finally, before we can proceed, we must address one additional issue for organizations. A focus on women in business in certainly not "new news."

What is missing is a true sense of urgency of the power of women as a business force.

Why is there no sense of urgency? The answer is hidden right in front of every business leader.

As I've admitted earlier, I'm a raving capitalist. This is one of the reasons I kicked off this chapter with one of America's best-known capitalists—Warren Buffet. If Mr. Buffett can see and articulate why women are so important today, how have so many organizations missed it? A number of years ago, I had an opportunity to meet Patricia Sellers, creator of the Fortune 50 most powerful women list. Once a year, Patricia hosts these women in a conference and gala event where the list of the most powerful women of the year is first announced.

When I asked Patricia, "do any men attend the event?" she laughed and said, "You know, that's funny. We invite a lot of men, but Warren Buffett is the only one who shows up."

Maybe this is one of the reasons he's a successful investor and one of the richest men in the world.

Male Gender Blindness—What Men Don't See

I mentioned earlier that the challenge to creating a sense of urgency for your women's strategy is hidden right in front of every business leader. In her breakthrough research, *The Sponsor Effect: Breaking Through the Last Glass Ceiling*, Sylvia Ann Hewlett uncovers some of these very issues. [10]

With a sample size of almost 3,000 U.S. business men and women, she discovered that male leaders don't see a lack of women in their organizations.

> **W** Fifty-six percent of men think women have made considerable progress over the past ten years.
>
> **W** Only 39 percent of women see it that way.

Male gender blindness refers to senior leaders looking around their organization and seeing "lots of women." They assume their companies are doing a good job in promoting and advancing women.

> *Unfortunately what they do not see*
> *are the titles and roles that these women hold.*
> *Women are largely stuck in staff functions, middle*
> *management, and administrative positions.*

This critical mass of women in organizations today are still in staff functions and are not holding P&L responsibility. They are not assigned to lead functions and make decisions in areas that are directly linked to the organization's top strategic initiatives. The reality is, women's roles in senior management have hardly changed in over thirty years. [11]

Percent of Women Occupying Top Management Positions

Human Resources	30%
Controller	14%
Marketing Officer	13%
Head of Sales	13%
CEO	10%
Chief Information Officer	8%

Women clearly aren't making it to the top. Despite decades of flooding into middle management, only one out of five is a senior leader today and fewer than one out of ten is a CEO. Hewlett believes that one of the things keeping women under the glass ceiling is the absence of male advocacy. High-performing women simply don't have the sponsorship they need to reach the top. [12]

When asked why they thought their companies were doing a good job in promoting and advancing women,

> **W** Fifty-eight percent of men say progress has been made by companies trying harder to promote women.
>
> **W** Fifty-seven percent of women credit their own performance and educational credentials and not the support of companies' male leaders as the reason for their own advancement.

As we can see, gender differences are quite apparent but rarely talked about.

Additionally, the research highlights that men are far less likely to recognize that gender bias exists.

> **W** Forty-nine percent of women believe gender bias is alive and well today.
>
> **W** Only twenty-eight percent of men agree.

Read this last fact slowly and out loud,

Almost one in two women in your organization believes that gender biases are alive today.

This obviously presents a huge organizational challenge. Are gender biases and sexism real issues in the workplace? Yes, of course they are. I will attest that every organization has elements of biases and sexism. That being said, I would like to believe that most men in most organizations are not consciously engaging in biased and sexist activities. What is important is to use these numbers and data to engage the organization in a meaningful business dialogue regarding the differences of men and women.

These two areas, "what companies are doing to promote women" and "the recognition of gender biases," represent important talking points for organizations to begin to drive change. Before we conclude this section I would like to bring up one more thing that "men aren't telling women" that hasn't been discussed yet.

In general,

Male leaders are uncomfortable even having conversations regarding gender differences with women. [13]

Though male leaders would never acknowledge this to women they are leading, men are ultimately concerned that they will be seen as insensitive, patronizing, or sexist if they even engage in conversation. [14]

Additionally, many of the men I have spoken with are actually afraid to have this conversation. At best they do not really see it being of value and at worst it could easily jeopardize their career and their livelihood. With all due respect to my HR and compliance brothers and sisters, men are scared to death that they will say or do the wrong thing if they attempt to engage in conversation around gender differences. Litigation and political correctness, along with seeing very little up-side have led men to not even choose to explore the topic.

This fear can often serve as an invisible and impenetrable barrier that organizations never discuss. Overcoming this fear is critical to moving the conversation forward. Enabling men to overcome this fear and become "ready-now" champions will be discussed in greater detail in Chapter 9.

To summarize, the three things men aren't telling women:

- "why things need to change"
- "what has to change"
- "who will drive change"

I added that organizations are lacking a sense of urgency that is compounded by the concept of Male Gender Blindness. I also added a fourth unspoken element, and that is,

"Why men are afraid to engage in this conversation."

These issues serve:

- To expose the need to have an integrated framework and see this as a business imperative
- To invoke a sense of urgency
- To uncover Male Gender Blindness
- To alleviate the fear that men face having a conversation regarding gender differences

This list provides a solid foundation for answering the question of "why things need to change."

Until now we've only discussed the strategic reasons for answering "why things need to change." In Chapter 3, I will complete this discussion by setting solid business case metrics and the need for complete organizational alignment. In Chapters 4 through 8, I will go into more detail to address "what has to change," and in Chapters 9 and 10, I'll address "who will drive change."

Summary Points of Chapter 2

- The three primary business reasons to create an Integrated Women's Leadership Strategy: to grow revenue, improve operating profit, and enhance company reputation. We must help the organization to visualize this opportunity so that it can be internalized by everyone.

- Organizations are lacking a sense of urgency regarding operationalizing their plans.

- Male Gender Blindness in organizations supports a belief that companies are making good progress when it is not.

- Men and women have significantly different points of view as to why women may or may not have advanced.

- Gender biases are real and must be talked about openly and honestly.

- Male leaders are afraid to engage in conversations regarding gender differences as they may be seen as insensitive, patronizing, or sexist if they even engage in conversation.

WHY WOMEN Readiness Assessment

1. Does your organization have a framework targeted to women that is designed to grow revenue, improve operating profits, and enhance company reputation?

2. Discuss the concept of Male Gender Blindness in your organization. As you look around the organization, what roles are the women in and how did they get there? One out of two women believes gender bias is still present in companies. What are you doing to combat gender bias in your organization?

3. Male leaders are uncomfortable having conversations regarding gender as they may be seen as insensitive, patronizing, or sexist. What is your organization doing to improve the ability of men to do a better job in providing feedback to women?

Deepening Your Learning

— *Book* —

The Strategist: Be the Leader Your Business Needs, Cynthia A. Montgomery

— *Online Article* —

"The Sponsorship Effect: Breaking Through the Last Glass Ceiling," Sylvia Ann Hewlett, Kerrie Peraino, Laura Sherbin, Karen Sumberg

— *Website* —

http://www.ywomen.biz

Chapter 3

The 80/80/80 Solution

**"The real drivers of the 'Post-American World'
won't be China . . . or India . . .
or Brazil – or any nation for that matter.**

The real drivers will be women."

— Muhtar Kent, Chairman and CEO,
The Coca-Cola Company at the World Economic Forum [15]

"Women are the primary purchases of . . . damn near everything!" This was the voice and indelible message that boomed through my computer speakers almost fifteen years ago. As I was viewing a webinar by Tom Peters on his new book, "Re-imagine!", I found myself captivated by what the future had in store. The voice speaking of the inevitable future quoted interesting research and presented story after story about the powerful convergence of multiple trends that would shape all things to come.

The voice spoke of the power of technology (yes, this was before Google was even born!), the importance of unleashing talent, the

43

seismic shift in the future workforce, and finally, that American women would represent $7 trillion in purchasing power.

Like most businessmen at the time, I had never really considered the magnitude of gender diversity. But with this new injection of insight brought by Mr. Peters, I finally understood the need to view diversity as a strategic imperative. It was an epiphany for me that immediately brought together the factors of revenue, talent, and productivity into a simple yet challenging equation.

The 80/80/80 Solution

The 80/80/80 Solution is the foundation for any organization wishing to build an Integrated Women's Leadership Strategy. Simply stated, these three elements will be used to demonstrate the importance of baseline metrics. The 80/80/80 Solution also becomes an easy visual mnemonic for the organization to understand as to why you're implementing an Integrated Women's Leadership Strategy.

The 80/80/80 Solution

> **W** 80+% Revenue - generated or influenced by women.
>
> **W** 80+% Talent - new entries into the workforce that are women and minorities.
>
> **W** 80+% Engagement - the aspirational engagement level of high-performing companies.

Let's explore each one of these in greater detail.

80+% Revenue

In a B2C (Business to Consumer) world, women are, in fact, the primary decision-makers and influencers of "damn near everything" bought and consumed in this country. In category after category, the numbers are actually quite staggering. [16]

W All consumer purchases: 85%	**W** Banking services: 89%
W Groceries: 93%	**W** Vacations: 92%
W Home furnishings: 94%	**W** Healthcare: 80%
W Home improvement projects: 80%	**W** Automobiles: 65% (influence 80%)

Now, I know what you're thinking, women do not buy 80 percent of homes or automobiles, and they certainly do not make up the bulk of the shoppers at Home Depot and Lowes (i.e., 80 percent of home-improvement projects). The operative word here is "influencer."

It's important for a company to distinguish the purchaser from the influencer.

A woman's influence goes far beyond her purchasing power.

For my male brethren reading this book, do you really think you had the final say in the house that you and your wife purchased? My guess is, your partner's criteria were significantly longer than yours. Okay, you may have been able to veto her decision, but you were certainly not going to buy a house that she was not happy with.

Home-improvement projects are another interesting phenomena. Eighty percent of home-improvement projects are actually initiated by women. I can honestly say I do not sit around on Saturday contemplating the need to redo the bathroom or the kitchen. No, in most households, the primary influencer of all the home fix-it projects is "her."

The B2C business case is overwhelmingly convincing, yet most companies have never done the hard work of quantifying what their true baseline revenue is when it comes to women. As a business leader, is your organization capable of articulating the baseline volume and growth volume by product category, business vertical, and customer segment as it relates to women?

A Game-Changing Realization

I was working with a rather large client organization in a traditional B2C model whose annual revenue growth hovered in the 3 to 4 percent range. In the midst of my work with them, the organization brought in a new CEO who threw down the challenge that the company would double its size in the next eight years.

You may be aware that in order to double the size of an organization, you need to grow at eight percent annually for eight years. That ambitious goal clearly required that the company undergo a significant business model shift away from historical patterns and force them to do the hard analytical work in identifying huge new avenues for growth. It took a strategic team working for weeks to quantify what would have to transpire to meet the new CEO's goals. The report from the team was a shocking revelation. For this client,

Over the course of the next eight years, 87 percent of the growth for the organization would come from women.

This represented a game-changing orientation for the company, as they realized they needed to get really, really good at understanding women. My question is, does your organization know what my client discovered? More importantly, can you and the leaders in your organization articulate and quantify your opportunity? We will continue this discussion on the B2C business case in Chapter 4, The $20 Trillion Niche.

A greater challenge is recognizing the impact that women are having in a B2B (Business to Business) world. Certainly, women are not the primary purchasers of railcars, jet engines, petrochemicals, or the other trillions of dollars' worth of items acquired by organizations in B2B exchanges. Yet, there's an unmistakable trend taking place in this world of business as well.

In September 2013, *Harvard Business Review* published a thought-leading piece on the importance of having women on your sales team in B2B environments. [17] A growing trend among companies, regardless of the industry, is the growing presence of women in procurement roles, and many with women as the team leader and final decision-maker.

Consider that,

> **W** Women hold about 50 percent of all managerial and professional positions.
>
> **W** Women represent 41 percent of employees with authority to make purchasing decisions.

The research shares insights into how companies are discovering real differences in how men and women as decision makers in procurement roles approach B2B deals. We've known from years of research that women tend to be "discovery-oriented" shoppers in the B2C marketplace and gather as much comprehensive information as possible on a product or service. Interestingly and understandably, this difference carries over into the B2B procurement process when it comes to how men and women make big-ticket purchases for their companies.

The findings from the study were eye-opening for B2B organizations.

- Women decision makers in B2B constantly have their antenna up when it comes to any sign of male condescension—whether coming from their male colleagues, clients, partners, or suppliers. As one female executive put it, "Men tend to have a fairly patronizing, 'pat-your-head approach' with female clients that they don't have with men."

- Women view a first meeting with a potential service provider as a chance to explore options with an expert resource while men see the event as a near-final stage in the process of narrowing down options and deciding on a vendor.

- Men view the RFP (request for proposal) process as defining the scope of an engagement and clarifying the rules of the game. Women, on the other hand, tend to view the RFP as a "useful guide that creates an opportunity for exploration with the prospective client."

Companies that are seeing the value in these differences are benefiting from the different line of sight women bring to the table—not better—just different, and quite often complementary to what men bring.

If your B2B sales force does not have women on it, you're missing out on a tremendous opportunity and probably losing out on big deals too. It may be that your mostly-male sales force doesn't know how to sell to women. We'll explore this concept further in Chapter 4, "The $20 Trillion Niche," when we talk about selling to men and selling to women.

80+% Talent

The demographics of our country are changing at a rapid pace. In Chapter 1, I mentioned that I would use the words "women" and "diversity" in a similar manner. This becomes necessary and critical as we attempt to discuss talent pools today. It is literally impossible to talk about talent without discussing two other macro trends, the impact of millennials and the representation of multi-cultural workers in the available talent pool.

Today as a macro number,

> **W** Nearly 85 percent of new entries into the workforce are represented by women and minorities. [18]

Let that sink in for a moment. This is obviously an astonishing number and the reason for organizations to sit up and take notice. That being said, it represents the percentage of the population that is turning eighteen today and in the future. The majority of this work group will not reach your doors for a few years. However, a significant percentage of the workforce is already here; and today's new workforce is significantly different than that of just fifteen years ago.

Many organizations talk about the diverse makeup of the new talent, yet have failed to move beyond the rhetoric and begin internalizing the trend. By 2018, the millennial generation—born between 1977 and 1992, will be the largest available workforce.

You may still be thinking that millennials are college-aged kids and it will be another ten years before they enter the work world.

Nothing could be further from the truth.

Millennials are now entering their thirties and this also includes a higher percentage of minorities than at any other time in history. Take note: the talent pipeline and middle management of your organization in less than five years—based on current U.S. representation—will look significantly different than it does today.

Not only does the current pipeline look significantly different than most of senior management today, but most managers and leaders have not been trained to deal with nuances of young, ultra-talented women or of the racial, ethnic, and cultural diversities flooding into your organizations and looking to belong.

The megatrend of women is already showing itself in the profile of today's college graduate.

If you are a knowledge-based company, women are definitely your future.

Since the 1980s, women have represented over well over 50 percent of college graduates in the United States. Today,

> **W**   Sixty percent of master's degrees and 58 percent of bachelor's degrees are being earned by women.
>
> **W**   Forty-five percent of MBA graduates and 62 percent of JD degrees in law are women. [19]

If you really want to know how big this impact is, do this research. Examine the major universities in your state and study the ratio of female to male enrollment. The statistics will stun you!

In my home state of Georgia, women's academic enrollment is greater than that of men in 22 of the 25 largest universities in the state, including the three largest schools. [20]

If you're looking for a young, smart, talented employee, chances are it's a woman.

This talent issue is also being complicated by another trend. Baby Boomers are leaving your workforce in droves. This mass exodus of Baby Boomers from the labor force compounds this pipeline transformation even more.

> **W** Every day, over 10,000 Baby Boomers are retiring and leaving the workforce. This is a trend that will continue every day in every company, for the next ten years! [21]

These employees, who are largely comprised of white males, make up a very large percentage of your employee base, especially at the senior-most levels. These are your key knowledge workers—your individual contributors, middle managers, thought leaders, and a sales force and field organization steeped in customer and client experience and selling skills.

Most engineering, technical, and scientific-based workers fall into this category as well. The amount of intellectual and institutional capital that will be leaving the workforce in the next ten years is incomprehensible. And the challenges for organizations will be to quickly replace and expand this knowledge of your products and your markets with the pipeline of existing talent.

This last issue creates an interesting paradox. I have worked with executive teams who say talent is "our number one priority." Yet, when you get the Divisional Vice President of Sales alone in one-on-one meeting, he's often willing to concede to you that talent is important and that he will of course support the executive agenda. However, he'll tell you in the same breath that delivering business results in the next six months—what he's being measured against right now—is the more pressing issue, and therefore takes precedence. Many on the front line clearly articulate their motivation in this simple response . . .

"Supporting talent long-term is critical, but I may not have a job in six months if I don't deliver results."

Thus the paradox: achieving results today versus investing in a pipeline.

His current, highly skilled knowledge pool of white men will be leaving him within the next five years, and chances are 85 percent of the replacement talent will be women and minorities.

This single reason, a long-term focus on talent, represents the critical need for all of the senior leadership team to engage in developing a diverse pipeline of talent and shepherding this process down to all levels of the organization. This also drives the sense of urgency to enable the next generation of talent to step forward.

Additionally, if this wasn't enough of a reason for getting serious about talent, here's one more issue on the horizon that complicates matters even further.

If you look at the curriculum at Harvard, Northwestern, Stanford, and many of the other major business schools in the nation, the overwhelming major of choice for today's business school student is Entrepreneurship. It appears many of these young, brightest, best-of-the-best are intending to start their own companies.

Said another way . . .

The best and brightest graduates today do not want to work for your organization.

Twenty years ago, freshly minted B-school grads wanted to be in sales at IBM, in brand management at Procter & Gamble, and in trade securities at Goldman Sachs. Today the last thing they want to do is work for a large, slow-to-change, slow-to-adapt, Fortune 500 company.

Incredible macro trends are converging that demonstrate the war for talent is real. The need to think differently about available talent, current talent, and future talent are reason enough to have a stand-alone dedicated people strategy. And as important as finding talent is, keeping it, motivating it, and engaging that talent is just as critical.

80+% Engagement

Engagement is not just a feel-good number but a true measure of productivity. High-performing companies today are striving for an 80 percent engagement rate. Unfortunately, many companies don't come even close to achieving that level of involvement, dedication, and loyalty.

The *2013 Gallup Poll on the State of the American Workplace* [22] found that,

A jaw-dropping 70 percent of full-time workers do not have an emotional connection to their work, meaning they only "go through the motions" to perform their jobs.

According to the Gallup study, here's how the mindset of your employees most likely breaks down:

> **W** One-third of your full-time workers are actively engaged and are considered committed, invested employees.
>
> **W** Over half (52 percent) of your workforce are non-engaged, emotionally absent at work, and basically putting in their time without energy or passion.
>
> **W** Eighteen percent are actively disengaged from their work and the organization, slowing down even further the productivity of the already unengaged, and potentially undermining the good work done by those who are engaged.

Despite the barriers to workplace equality such as hiring, pay, and promotion-bias, women report to being more engaged with their work and workplace than men.

More than thirty years ago, Gallup pioneered the concept of the engagement survey and only recently began to track the differences in gender ratings on engagement. Gallup doesn't explain the gender gap in workplace engagement, but some of its findings may suggest the reason why.

> **W**   Thirty-nine percent of employees who work off-site are slightly more engaged than their on-site-full-time counterparts.

This suggests that flexible work arrangements—to attend to family responsibilities or other important needs—improves women's involvement and dedication with their companies.

This releases pressure and stress and pays un-captured dividends to employers with engaged, committed personnel—not to mention additional hours worked.

> **W**   Gallup found that remote workers put in an average four additional hours per week than their non-remote counterparts.

An additional reason that women may feel more emotionally engaged stems from the benefits of flextime. The Gallup poll found that flextime produces the greatest effect on employees' overall well-being when compared with other incentives such as vacation days and reduced hours.

The survey results are even more startling . . .

> **W**   Forty-five percent of working adults surveyed are willing to give up some percentage of their salary to achieve flexibility.

More and more, women and men are feeling challenged by the pressures of a demanding work life and hectic personal life, and surveys are beginning to reflect this in the value professionals of all ages place on workplace flexibility. Workplace flexibility is not just "a nice to do," it is a critical to do if you want to retain and engage men and women today!

The Non-Engaged Workforce

This trend of low engagement is not going unnoticed in major organizations. The challenge is most leaders don't know what to do about it. Deloitte's *2014 Global Human Capital Trends* research reported in conjunction with *Forbes* Magazine,

> **W** Seventy-eight percent of business leaders rate retention and engagement as urgent or important, but only 15 percent believe they are ready to address it.

These leaders see talent and the engagement of that talent as major challenges to growth. Some of the key conclusions in this "wake-up-call" survey of over 2,500 CEOs and senior executives across ninety countries include:

- Performance management is broken.

- Replace "rank and yank" with coaching and development.

- Move from compliance to diversity and inclusion as a business strategy.

- Shift from talent metrics to non-biased talent assessment.

- Move from talking about growth of talent to internalizing and strategizing for it.

My approach is not to reflect on engagement as a nice thing to do, but for you to take it up as a real-time action plan to drive and focus productivity on your most critical asset—your employees. And as with many elements of an Integrated Women's Leadership Strategy, high engagement is not merely "a women's" issue, but a total employee workforce strategy that not only serves your company's bottom-line interests but also the personal interests of all your employees.

At the end of the day, it's no coincidence that the companies that consistently rate as having the highest engaged workforce are also the companies with the highest level of "female/family friendly" benefits such as flextime, telecommuting, extended maternity leaves, on-site day care, and dozens of other programs that allow companies to get the best out of all their talent.

I want your three takeaways from this exploration into talent and engagement to be this:

1. Companies need to track recruitment, advancement, retention, and engagement, and view them as drivers of operating profit.

2. Women, on average tend to be more engaged than men for a variety of reasons, such as their company's reputation, and in turn, are more apt to engage others—if their contribution is valued.

3. In the end, the need for engagement is not a men/women thing, but if a company has "female/family friendly" programs, all of their employees are more engaged—and not just a fraction.

Creating Your 80/80/80 Business Case

These three elements of Talent, Revenue, and Engagement make up the foundational business case for our model. While it is nice to talk in esoteric terms such as 80/80/80, it's much harder for organizations to measure it.

Now, the hard work begins. For each of these elements, we must go through a business analysis process. We need to examine both current state and future state.

While your own analysis needs to be tailored to your specific industry and organization, there are few general questions that can be asked immediately.

Revenue

1. What is the current total revenue pie available with a focus on women?

2. What percentage are we capturing?

3. What is the revenue/opportunity gap?

4. How much can we capture with available products and services?

5. What are the additional products and services that are needed to grow our business and how much will those efforts yield in the next twelve to eighteen months and beyond?

Talent

1. What does our current workforce look like by time of service, gender, race, age, and ethnicity?

2. How does our current workforce break down the higher up the organization we go?

3. Are we adequately attracting and retaining new talent to replace retiring knowledge workers?

4. From where are we sourcing our new talent and are our efforts undertaken with a true "lens" on gender?

5. What is our retention and advancement rate by gender? How does rate change the higher up the organization we go?

Engagement

1. Do we currently have an engagement strategy in place?

2. Have we measured engagement by gender, race, tenure, and ethnicity?

3. How are we holding managers accountable for increasing engagement?

4. Does our reputation inside and out encourage or discourage engagement and why?

5. Do we know what programs, policies, and procedures are adding to and detracting from the commitment and passionate involvement of our employees?

This can often be a challenging process and as I work with organizations it can be very frustrating. The 80/80/80 Business Case may be aspirational for your company and that is okay. Starting on this work becomes the foundational element to crafting a multi-year strategy.

Having completed this assessment, we can then return to our strategic framework. The 80/80/80 Business Case on our framework becomes your current state foundational assessment. Having established a baseline, we can now look at opportunity gap analysis and future state activity.

YWomen Integrated Women's Leadership Framework

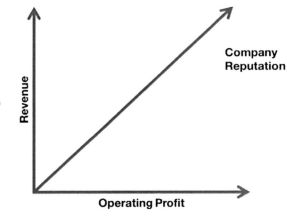

Company Reputation

Revenue

The YWomen 80/80/80 Business Case

- 80+% of purchasing decisions made by Women

- 80+% of new entries to the workforce are Women & Minorities

- 80+% is the Engagement Goal for High Performing Companies

Operating Profit

If your organization successfully completes the activities above and candidly answers the questions on Revenue, Talent, and Engagement, I guarantee you that you're well ahead of most of the organizations in the Fortune 500. This assessment, done properly, should provide you a host of opportunity gap assessments and SWOT (Strengths, Weaknesses, Opportunities, Threats) analyses. This is the critical work that is necessary in order to set a baseline with which to build success. Having now established your solid business case, we can then begin to look at the Five Key Business Elements, including Sales and Marketing, Field Operations, HR, Senior Leadership, and Corporate Communications.

Leveraging the Five Key Business Elements

These key business elements all directly correspond to key organizational functions that you already have in place. As we look at incorporating these into the framework, we can take a deeper examination of each element's role within the business.

Marketing and Operations

As we look at our revenue axis, we know that there are only two levers that generate revenue in organizations. One is marketing. Though not a revenue driver in and of itself, it's certainly one of the key business elements that support driving revenue. The other is sales and field operations. The goal of this step is to conduct an opportunity gap assessment (similar to the example in Chapter 2) and look at the incremental revenue that can be generated by properly leveraging women as consumers and customers.

These two levers become the foundation for Chapters 4 and 5 on The $20 Trillion Niche and The Field Factor. The important element at this point is to remember you will be putting measures and metrics in place for these elements to drive accountability throughout the organization. Without doing this hard work of determining the opportunity gaps through measure and metrics, this work will not be seen as valued by the organization.

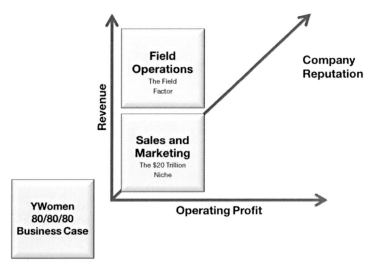

YWomen Integrated Women's Leadership Framework

Human Resources and Senior Leadership

We will now look at our operating profit/horizontal axis. This is where we examine opportunity cost savings through effective talent management and increased engagement. Again . . .

> *This is a hard metric discussion,*
> *not a "feel-good" HR discussion.*

In addition to hard metrics, we also should examine the need to embed your women's strategy into all of HR's processes. Everything from selection, to performance management, to compensation needs to have an element of the connection to a broader women's strategy.

Finally, as we look to the upper right quadrant we can now see the role of senior leadership and the need for an integrated scorecard "owned" by your executive team. All of these elements are critical for success, but only by having the senior leadership team directly involved and committed, with each function owning a portion of the success, can we be truly successful. These two levers will be explored in depth in Chapter 6 when we discuss The HR Paradox and Chapter 7 where we examine The Leadership Imperative.

YWomen Integrated Women's Leadership Framework

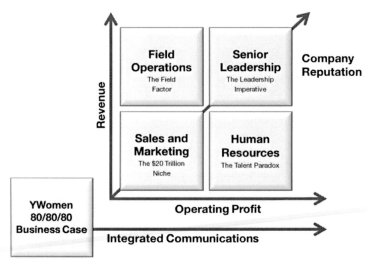

Company Reputation

Our fifth lever then becomes managing Company Reputation. In Chapter 2 this was mentioned as both a "why to do this work" and a "how to do this work." This critical business outcome will be discussed in Chapter 8.

Integrated Communications

Finally having now built an integrated framework, we add one additional piece. The final key element is the role of an Integrated Communications Plan, for both your internal and external audiences. The key to complete organizational commitment is every element of your communications strategy must be reviewed and integrated with the business case for your women's strategy. There is a critical need to get this right. This helps the organization to answer the question, "Why are we doing this?"

An integrated external communications plan is critical to telling your story to consumers, customers, perspective employees, and investors. It's the final vector that cuts across the entire model. It's a comprehensive plan that takes into account the strategic roles of all of your communications, including advertising, public relations, and social media. It combines them to provide clarity of message, consistency of message, and maximum communication impact.

Finally, it is critical to your senior leadership team. Internally with employees and externally with key stakeholders, does your CEO and senior leadership team have the succinct sound bites to tell the organization why we are doing "this women's thing?" Do they own the message and is it in their words or just corporate speak? The organization will know in a nanosecond if something is genuine or not. CEO and senior leader commitment form the basis of your integrated communications plan.

We have answered the burning question of "why" we need to develop an Integrated Women's Leadership Strategy. This work has helped us to begin to craft a written measureable plan that can move from concept to implementation. In Part Two of the book, we will take a deeper dive into the five key elements and explore the "what has to change" portion of the question.

Summary Points from Chapter 3

- The 80/80/80 Solution comprised of Baseline Revenue, Current Talent Base, and Current Engagement levels combine to become the foundational business case for organizations wishing to build an Integrated Women's Leadership Strategy.

- Women buy or influence over 80 percent of all B2C products and companies need to understand the significant role that they play as not just consumers but influencers.

- In the B2B space, women are redefining the rules and processes for procurement.

- Today, over 80 percent of new entries into the workforce are represented by women and minorities. And by 2018, this millennial generation—born between 1977 and 1992, will be the largest available workforce.

- Seventy-eight percent of business leaders rate retention and engagement as urgent or important, but only 15 percent believe they are ready to address it.

- As with many elements of an Integrated Women's Leadership Strategy high engagement is not merely "a women's issue." It's a total employee workforce strategy that not only serves your bottom-line interests, but also the personal interests of all your employees.

- All functional business areas must be addressed to obtain complete organizational alignment including the need to align all company communication elements.

WHY WOMEN Readiness Assessment

1. Regarding revenue, can your organization at all levels articulate your baseline and incremental revenue and profit goals of its women's strategy? What is the current total revenue pie available to you with a focus on women? What percentage are we capturing and what is the revenue/opportunity gap?

2. Regarding talent, what does your organization look like from top to bottom regarding gender, age, and ethnicity? What will your organization look like in five years? How are you capturing the intellectual knowledge of the boomers who will be retiring shortly?

3. Regarding engagement, does your organization currently have an engagement strategy in place? Are you measuring engagement by gender, race, tenure, and ethnicity? How are you holding managers accountable for increasing engagement?

Deepening Your Learning

— *Book* —

The Perfect Human Capital Storm: Workplace Challenges & Opportunities in the 21st Century, Edwin L. Mourino-Ruiz, Ph.D.

— *Online Article* —

"2014 Global Human Capital Trends," Deloitte in conjunction with *Forbes* Magazine

— *Website* —

http://www.aon.com

Part 2: Leveraging Critical Business Functions

Chapter 4

The $20 Trillion Niche

"Women are females first and consumers second. For marketers, knowing your audience as women must be accomplished before you can begin to understand them as consumers."

—Bridget Brennan, *Why She Buys* [23]

"Doesn't the Dri-Weave feel softer?" I was standing in a grocery store aisle in Marquette, Michigan, and had just poured blue water into an Always Maxi-Pad and a competitor's Maxi-Pad. I was a sales rep at the time, working for Procter & Gamble, and we were introducing Always feminine napkins with the newly patented Dri-Weave lining.

As part of the demonstration, I would grasp the hand of the buyer for the feminine napkin department and have him or her touch it. In the grocery industry in those days, mostly men were in charge of ordering all of the products in the store, including feminine napkins. After seven previous demonstrations to male buyers, my eighth sales presentation was to a woman.

As I broke into my rote presentation and before I could even take her hand, she looked me in the eye and said,

"Softer? Really? Have you ever worn one?"

Of course, she was right. In fact, as much as I enjoyed working for Procter & Gamble, introducing feminine napkins was clearly a low point of my career. Don't get me wrong, P&G has always been amazingly proactive in its efforts to market to women. Yet, like most every other company in those days, P&G had over a 90 percent male sales force conducting its product introductions, and this clearly did not make sense to me. Though I would not start YWomen for another twenty-five years, this particular day was etched in my memory.

How many organizations today are still not equipped to deal with women as their primary source of revenue? Said another way, does your organization, its marketing department, your advertising agency, and your sales force truly grasp and understand women? More importantly . . .

Has your organization, marketing department, advertising agency, and sales force moved from conceptualizing the idea of women to internalizing it?

This is a challenging question to ask if you are a non-marketer. Few non-marketers ever question their company's marketing efforts. The goal of this chapter is not to challenge your marketing people but to engage them in a deeper conversation regarding revenue and women that can be shared and linked with the total organizational strategy. As this is an organizational "how-to" book, I want you to focus on a breadth of compelling elements that you need to understand in order to support a truly integrated model.

The $20 Trillion Niche

It's virtually impossible to comprehend the enormity of the global buying power of women. We throw around figures such as $20 trillion globally and $7 trillion in the United States, however, until your organization has done the hard work to evaluate the size and significance of the niche for your company, this chapter will mean very little to you.

My hope is that you completed the exercises in Chapter 3, answering the questions related to Revenue, Talent, and Engagement, and that you've formulated a clear vision of how important women are. If you haven't done the work, perhaps this chapter will encourage you to go back and take another look at those questions.

According to SheEconomy.com, women account for 85 percent of all consumer purchases spanning virtually everything from groceries and home improvements to automobiles and health care: [24]

W All consumer purchases: 85%	**W** Banking services: 89%
W Groceries: 93%	**W** Vacations: 92%
W Home furnishings: 94%	**W** Health care: 80%
W Home improvement projects: 80%	**W** Automobiles: 65% (influence 80%)

Moreover, women also purchase/influence:

W 66% of personal computers

W 61% of consumer electronics

W 80% of home maintenance

W 65% of service at car dealerships

W 45% of all light trucks and SUVs

In her book, *The Power of the Purse: How Smart Businesses Are Adapting to the World's Most Important Consumer—Women*, [25] Fara Warner challenges companies to answer some thought-provoking questions:

1. Do you have a stereotypical view of women consumers that hasn't changed in more than a year?

2. Do you still think of women as a minority?

3. Are you afraid to be the first in your industry to focus on women and if you do, you think it will turn off male consumers?

4. Do you think one ad campaign or marketing message will work on all women?

5. Do you ever wish the whole idea of gender would just go away?

The data is overwhelming, which clearly demonstrates the power and influence of women in virtually every category. There have been hundreds of books, articles, and conferences devoted to educating organizations on the importance of women. My encouragement is for you to delve into your own data, for I know you will find the statistics overwhelming.

It All Starts with Marketing

I'm not a classically trained marketer, but then my guess is that neither are most of the readers of this book. I do not intend to turn you into marketers, but to trigger your curiosity. As senior leaders of your organization, you need to ask thought-provoking questions of your corporate marketing department and implement measures and metrics as a portion of your strategy for delivering business results for women. Why? Because believe it or not most marketers don't understand women.

> **W** Ninety-one percent of women said that advertisers don't understand them. [26]

I will be the first to admit that creating great marketing and advertising is significantly more of an art than that of a science. For every amazing campaign that hits home, there are hundreds more that miss the mark or lay dead on the creative director's floor. The key to today's most effective campaigns, new products, and line extensions is in venturing into the psyche of the female consumer. And nothing could be more challenging.

The challenge is, you cannot homogenize women, whether it is a single female, mom, grandmother, shopper, or consumer. Marketers attempt to put women in tidy and efficient boxes but unfortunately this is not effective. [27]

If we know one thing, it is that every woman's life is unique, multidimensional, and often challenging. To be truly successful, organizations need to begin by examining the two major intersecting points of her life—her economic status and her household status.

In its study, "The Female Economy," *Harvard Business Review* surveyed more than 12,000 women from more than forty geographies including a variety of income levels and various walks of life. [28] The following chart clearly demonstrates some of the complexities of identifying women as a marketing subset. Moreover, few women fall into just one type. For instance, married fast trackers with children are likely, at some point in their lives, to also fall into the pressure cooker category.

Six Key Female Consumer Segments

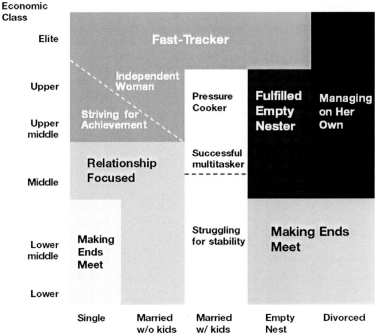

As you study this diagram, ask yourself, to whom are your products targeted and where do they fit on this chart?

Let's peer a little deeper into this segment with two other lenses that need to be used to view this data. First, we need to differentiate women as both shopper and consumer. While we can think of many items that she is the consumer of, she plays a much broader role as the shopper.

Does your marketing department differentiate shopper from consumer? Bridget Brennan, author of *Why She Buys* says,

> *"In addition to buying for themselves, women buy on behalf of husbands, partners, kids, colleagues, adult children, friends, relatives, elderly parents, in-laws, their businesses, and even their kids' friends, to name just a few. If somebody somewhere needs a gift, chances are there's a woman thinking about it; tracking it down; wrapping it; making sure it's accompanied by a personal message and then arriving to the person on the appointed day. I sometimes think entire industries would collapse overnight if women stopped being so thoughtful. Consider the impact to the greeting card industry alone."* [29]

The next important lines of sight are that of youth and multiculturalism. I mentioned this megatrend earlier and it is not merely restricted to talent. Marketers in a tendency to compartmentalize and homogenize women, often let these two trends go unnoticed. Farnaz Wallace author of *The New World Marketplace: How Women, Youth and Multiculturalism are Shaping Our Future,* frames it this way,

"While most organizations have targeted the classic stay-at-home wife/working mother of two, nothing could be further from the truth. Millennial women are nothing like their mothers. Millennials strive for connection and relationships on an individual basis versus trying to fit into a social norm. They are about individuality and uniqueness. Additionally one-third of the millennial generation was born to single unwed mothers. While many may be in a committed relationship, it is certainly a different environment. This changes their point of view on being a woman today." [30]

Farnaz goes on to point out that marketers most often miss out on the multicultural effect.

"Currently 36 percent of the U.S. population is nonwhite, which means one out of every three female shoppers is multicultural. So even in companies that do target women it is rare that they would allocate one third of their female marketing budget to multicultural women. Shockingly, Hispanic women, African American women, and Asian women, actually spend and control a greater percentage of the buying income for the household."

If we do the math on this one megatrend alone, 33 percent of $7 trillion, reveals that . . .

> **W** In the United States, multicultural women represent approximately $2.31 trillion.

Has your organization applied a female multicultural and generational lens on all the elements of your marketing mix and on your most successful products? For deeper understanding of how to apply these concepts let's examine who is doing an effective job in tailoring its marketing to women.

Who's Doing it Well

Sandy Sabean is the Chief Creative Officer of Womenkind, a New York-based agency that specializes in marketing to women. In her opinion, a number of Consumer Packaged Goods (CPGs) companies are really hitting the mark.

> *"Proctor & Gamble has really hit the mark understanding the psyche of female consumers as strong empowered women. Pantene's 'Not Sorry' Video Tells Women To Stop Apologizing So Much. This is an inspired and creative way to express this insight."* [31]

P&G also hits the mark for its campaign on mothers and the Olympics, connecting two very powerful icons. Other consumer package goods also score well. Unilever and Dove's "Real Beauty" ads have been running for over ten years and still deliver a very authentic message.

And while we may expect CPGs to get this right we really need to expect other industries that derive as much economic value from women to also raise their game. Remember this is not just about creating effective marketing, it's using your marketing function as a key driver of a broader Integrated Women's Leadership Strategy.

It's All about Her

Target Corporation is one such retailer that truly understands and caters to women. You can see it in the layout of their stores, the contemporary designer apparel, and even the low mom-friendly height of their gondola shelves. This is not just about wanting to attract women, it is truly about a cultural DNA that knows women's expectations and serves their needs. From the associates at the store level to corporate officers, no one refers to Target shoppers as "consumers" or even "guests." Everything is about "her." You notice it in the way they communicate with each other, strategize with their vendors, and speak to it in all their internal and external communications. Spend a few minutes with any Target executive and is very clear they are all about women.

> ***Everything in their culture is about "her" and "she."***
> ***What is "her shopping experience, what is she thinking."***

Another company that is redefining its DNA is Nike. While Nike might make you think of Air Jordans or Tiger Woods, Nike is very quickly evolving. In late 2014 Nike opened its first women's-only store and has plans for a lot more. Why? Nike expects its women's business to grow to $7 billion annually by 2017 and outpace the sales of menswear! [32]

Why are some companies grasping the ideas while others have not?

As a point of application, let's examine two industries, financial services and automotive, to illustrate what I believe are disconnects with marketplace reality. I chose these two particular sectors because they are clear examples of opportunities hidden in plain view and as research shows they are very misunderstood by marketers.

> **W** Eighty-four percent of women feel misunderstood by investment marketers.
>
> **W** Seventy-four percent of women feel misunderstood by automotive marketers.

Financial Services and Prime-Time Women

If you are in the financial services, wealth management, or insurance industries, please read the following number slowly and out loud:

Seventy-five percent of the nation's financial wealth is controlled by women. [33]

Marti Barletta is author of *PrimeTime Women: How to Win the Hearts, Minds, and Business of Boomer Big Spenders*, [34] and I cannot think of a better term to use than hers: "Primetime Women are ages 50-plus." Once the college bills are out of the way and children have launched their own careers and households, the discretionary spending power of fifty-plus women soars to 250 percent of what the average person spends. Women are the primary buyers for computers, cars, banking, financial services, and a host of other big-ticket items. And their *primetime* is not only in consumer purchasing but . . .

Women age fifty and older control a cumulative net worth of $19 trillion.

Said another way, if you're only looking at men as your financial services clients, you're focusing all your resources on a mere 25 percent of the investing market. Yet, this is where most of the financial institutions in this country are still converging. The financial services, wealth management, and insurance industries are dominated by male sales and marketing representatives who have little to no clue as to the unique needs of women who control the other three-fourths of that pie. If you're in the wealth management or insurance game, you've got a staggering challenge ahead of you, gaining and retaining clients with a predominately male sales force focused primarily on transacting with men.

Most financial institutions now acknowledge that . . .

> **W** Seventy percent of women will switch financial advisors when their husbands die. [35]

Once a woman is on her own, she isn't satisfied or mollified by standard performance reporting or the occasional nine holes of golf. A woman likes to feel that her financial advisor is taking the time to educate her about the financial planning process and its opportunities, and is responding to her personal needs.

She doesn't want someone who will assume her goals are the same as those set by her late husband. "Let me just continue to take care of your investments," she is often and patronizingly told. "I know your finances and I know your goals. We'll just continue along the same path your husband had taken."

Like men, women want to be educated, understand fee structures, and have advisors who are trying to help them comprehend their full financial picture. Instead of a sales pitch, they want to be taught about products in a language they understand so they can have a sense of urgency and control. Unlike men, they don't want a transaction-oriented person handling their nest egg, but a relational advisor who is respectful and responsive. Financial services firms that continue to ignore women's needs should do so at their own peril.

This is a compounding opportunity for those companies within the financial services industry who can overcome their market blind spot and embrace the future.

> **W** Many Boomer women will experience a double inheritance windfall, from both parents and husband. Estimates range in the $12 to $40 trillion range. [36]

Another key factor to consider is that you may never find or talk to these boomer women, especially the 70 percent who drop their financial planner when their spouse dies. The vast majority will select their next financial advisor based on advice from their colleagues, family, and friends. Women shopping for financial advisors are not going to be steered by any type of mailing, television commercial, or other marketing hype. They're left uninformed and often offended.

> *She is typically not going to answer a roto-call, advertisement, or an offer for a free steak dinner. Instead, she'll turn to the person she trusts most in the world, her best friend.*

The challenge is that if you don't currently have a reputation for having women as your focus, present in your field force, and as loyal clients, it's going to be very difficult attract new ones with what you're currently doing—overlooking the needs of 75 percent of the market.

Playing a Game or Getting a Root Canal

Does anyone really enjoy the car buying process? Not surprisingly, many men still enjoy the combative negotiation process that still exists. When men and women were asked to word associate around the term "negotiating," men likened it to doing battle, playing a game, or engaging in "I win, you lose." Women, on the other hand, associate negotiating with "getting a root canal." Yet women themselves make 65 percent of new car purchases in this country and influence upwards of 80 percent of all vehicle purchases. [37]

If you were to ask women their number one least liked experience in life, buying a car is often at the top of their list. How can an industry filled with successful, long-standing automakers get this entire process from beginning to end so wrong?

At a recent Marketing to Women conference, a woman volunteered this story.

From a design standpoint, if automakers truly gave a damn about women, they would start by designing the car around the most important element in my life, my purse. [38]

When I asked her to tell me more, she said that a woman carries her life in her purse. It holds her cell phone, checkbook, wallet, credit card, emergency items, Tide stick, cosmetics, and everything else that she finds important for her in her day-to-day life.

The woman concluded by saying, "I drive a Lexus 400 SUV. They've come as close as I've seen to having a place for my purse. It's a big open area on the floor between the seats, so maybe they were thinking about me."

If automakers really knew how important a purse was to a woman's life, they might do a better job of redesigning a key feature of their cars. The engineering and design divisions of companies in this enormous industry are another example of departments deep within the operations of the business with mindsets that still don't understand and cater to women's needs.

While volumes of books could be written about how dissatisfied women are with their experience in buying cars, I believe the most important selling environment, which is largely male, typically transactional—and not by any stretch of the imagination relational enough—is the dealership showroom.

New research from Women-Drivers.com shows that,

> **W** Three in ten women are apprehensive about shopping for car at their local dealership.
>
> **W** Twenty percent consider the experience "downright overwhelming." [39]

Most women today would rather buy a car online than deal with car salesmen who tend to be aggressive closers, don't provide all the information women are looking for, and quite frankly don't take women shoppers seriously.

Forward-thinking car dealers are beginning to understand that if they cannot immediately establish rapport and trust, she will buy her car elsewhere.

Establishing trust in what they view as an unwelcoming and unreceptive environment is the number one thing that matters to women; price is secondary!

This is not just true for the auto industry. Every industry needs to reread the statement above. Women are actually willing to pay more for your goods or service if you have developed a trusting relationship with her by demonstrating dignity, respect, and integrity. This issue of trust will be examined a number of times throughout the book and how elusive the opportunity may actually be.

Can the financial services and automobile industries, and a host of others, truly change their DNA? Of course they can, and it's already starting to take root. A handful of companies are doing a good job in demonstrating their awareness of the buying power of women and showing their commitment to this dominant buying segment. Others should stand up and take notice, for the first in will reap huge rewards.

Your Agency, Your Customer, Your Sales Force

What does your agency look like?

Many executives I talk to say, "I have great people in my marketing department. In fact, a significant percentage of the people in my marketing department are women. How can we possibly be missing this opportunity?"

Well, the answer may surprise you. I know that I've just laid out a dizzying array of facts and figures on the many elements regarding marketing to women, but here is one more amazing fact for you to ponder:

> **W** Eighty-nine percent of the creative directors at advertising agencies are men! [40]

I know what you're thinking: it's not 1960 and agencies are not run as those depicted in the popular cable series, *Mad Men*. True to a point. The ad agency world today is indeed dominated by women. The majority of entry-level and middle management positions—from account management, to media buying, to research, knowledge, and insights—are staffed by women.

Yet when it comes to working with the C-level and marketing departments of companies creating the products and advertising objectives, chances are a male director will be the lead contact with final say on those campaign objectives and creative strategies.

As Kat Gordon, one of the "Top 10 Women to Watch" in *Advertising Age* and founder of The 3% Conference puts it . . .

> *"There are only three consumer categories where men dominate purchases, yet agencies still talk about 'women's accounts' as mops and makeup. The truth is that women are the superset, not the subset, and the rate at which women are amassing wealth and exerting influence is unprecedented. Yet the work that is supposed*

to motivate them springs almost entirely from a male perspective. The advertising business is a $33 billion industry. Misunderstanding female consumers, from a business perspective is sheer lunacy." [41]

Gordon couldn't be more right on the mark. Given that women control 85 percent of all consumer purchase decisions and represent only 11 percent of creative directors, you can expect a mismatch of objectives, targets, messages, and expectations—and female consumers clearly believe there are. This issue is beginning to gain a compounding effect as customers are examining their own suppliers to begin to insure they are responding to the needs of the marketplace.

Your Customer May be Putting You on Notice

The composition of your agency and account teams is not being unnoticed by customers. Companies are now beginning to hold their suppliers accountable. Walmart is using its corporate muscle to support women. In 2011, they launched the global Walmart women's initiative. [42]

By the end of 2016, five years into their cultural transformation, Walmart's further-reaching goals are to:

1. Source $20 billion from Women Business Owners in the United States and internationally.

2. Hire and train 60,000 women for its suppliers, factories, and farms.

3. Empower 200,000 women internationally through its Retail Training Programs.

4. Invest $100 million in grants toward women's economic empowerment across the globe.

5. **Increase gender diversity among its major suppliers with more than $1 billion in sales.**

The design of this five-pronged strategy is to help them grow their presence in local communities and recruit, retain, and develop female talent. Their overall initiative has gotten a lot of press, yet the one element that's not being talked about a lot is item **Number Five**. Though not often mentioned, this is an absolute game changer. We are now witnessing one of the largest companies in the world making a statement that in essence says,

If you are going to do business with Walmart, you need to increase the number of women calling on us.

This speaks volumes for Walmart's commitment to women. More importantly, once the world's largest retailer makes this kind of declaration, how long will it be before other major companies act in a similar fashion? Most organizations today have women sales forces that are well less than 40 percent women and minorities.

What is your organization going to do when its largest customer says that it wants you to increase the number of women and minorities calling on them?

So let's summarize where we are. Let's assume you've gotten your organization to frame a new mindset around women and you've started to internalize the need for change with your leadership team. You've worked with your marketing department to be laser-focused on your biggest trends and you've even gotten your agency on board, and they're staffing up on your account in a gender proportionate manner to meet your company's needs.

What could possibly be missing?

The Betrayal of Marketing by Sales

What do you get when you combine one of Coca-Cola's most iconic brand names with one of the fastest-growing segments in the beverage industry? The most anticipated new energy drink launch of 2006 – Tab Energy. While Tab Energy shares the Tab brand name, it is not a cola. It is a completely new energy drink created especially for women. The deliciously crisp and lightly carbonated pink beverage is sugar-free, with only five calories per 10.5 ounce can. Tab Energy will be available in eye-catching, fashionably pink cans and four-packs—Bevnet News, 2006 [43]

I believe Tab Energy was actually one of the products that marketing got right. The energy drink category in 2006 was exploding, and while it was largely perceived as a male-dominated segment, consumer research demonstrated that a significant portion of energy drinkers were women. Up until the introduction of Tab Energy, the category was filled with ultra-macho names such as Monster and Rockstar. Tab still carried incredible brand equity among women, and Tab Energy would be the first female-oriented, great tasting, low-calorie energy drink. It made perfect marketing sense and for Coke it presented an exciting marketing opportunity.

Within five years of its introduction, the brand would peak, fizzle, and be discontinued. [44] I believe one of the contributing problems was that . . .

The largely male sales force had trouble understanding how to uniquely sell the benefits of this product.

Like my experience of men selling feminine napkins for Procter & Gamble, I believe the Coca-Cola route salesmen may have lacked the ability to articulate the unique and intrinsic values of products not targeted to them. Marketing to women is not easy; selling to women is even harder.

In my first book, *Selling to Men Selling to Women,* I articulate the blind spots that men face when selling to women and that women face in selling to men. To help illustrate these blind spots, let me summarize a few of the key points made in my book in understanding gender dynamics in the sales process:

- Men tend to approach buying and selling as a left-brain, transactional process while women approach buying and selling as a whole-brain exercise. As a result, women tend to approach sales as a relationship rather than as a transaction. Sales people, regardless if they're men or women, must be highly skilled in adapting to either gender and in any situation.

- Men's inclination is to start selling from a transactional standpoint. It's how they've always done it and they may not know how to adapt in a relational sale.

- Women communicate three times the amount of information both verbally and nonverbally than men do. Most men are unprepared when female buyers ask three times the questions. Why do they ask so many questions? Because, in their reasoning, they're not just seeking a solution but searching for the best one and looking to establish a relational exchange.

- Women tend to nod their head to acknowledge the receipt of information. This doesn't mean they're agreeing as men often indicate with their nod. Women are just confirming with you that they're listening and want you to continue.

- Men need to be acutely attuned of a woman's nonverbal communication. Men have an ability to disrespect women without even opening their mouths. Building trust in the relationship upfront is the most important element of the relational sales process.

- Women want men to look them in the eye when they sell to them as a sign of connectivity and trustworthiness. They have an instinctual ability to read meta-messages around the eyes and lips—something men are typically not equipped to notice. Men tend not to make long and direct eye contact, for it may indicate aggressiveness. A man's failure to look a women in the eye is interpreted by her as a sign of mistrust.

- When men are selling to men and get a "no," this often means "bring me another solution." When a woman says no, she actually means no. By that stage of the sales process her whole-brain buying model has most likely explored every possible option and your attempt to "handle" her objections is probably not going to change her mind.

- When selling to a man and a woman at the same time, the seller needs to be attentive to connecting with her first, and not in a patronizing way, to build trust, establish rapport, and demonstrate respect.

Tab Energy is merely one example of a list of hundreds of products targeted to women that have failed for one reason or another. Was it the organization's fault for not evolving their DNA? Was it marketing research that dropped the ball? Did the agency do its job? Did the sales force lack the knowledge and ability to speak knowingly to the key user benefits?

The challenge to get this right is daunting. Yet the stakes are too incredibly high for organizations to continue to ignore or assume they have a handle on the $20 trillion global opportunity.

Summary Points from Chapter 4

- Women today account for 85 percent of all consumer purchases spanning virtually everything from groceries and home improvements to automobiles and health care.

- The key to today's most effective campaigns, new products, and line extensions is in deeply reaching into the psyche of the female consumer. And nothing could be more challenging.

- Every woman's life is unique, multidimensional, and often challenging. To be truly successful, organizations need to begin by examining the two major intersecting points of her life—her economic status and her household status.

- Companies need to differentiate women as both shopper and consumer. The next important lines of sight are that of youth and multiculturalism. In our tendency to compartmentalize and homogenize women, these two elements often go unnoticed.

- Only 11 percent of creative directors are women.

- Large customers are starting to ask for more of a gender diverse representation in their account teams.

- Marketing to women is not easy; selling to women is even harder. Men approach selling from a Transactional Model. Women tend to buy in a Relational style that most men are not adequately trained to deal with.

WHY WOMEN Readiness Assessment

1. Does your organization, its marketing department, your agency, and your sales force truly grasp and understand women at a deep level? Does your organization see women as the majority driver of your business or are they classified as a niche?

2. Examine your advertising agency. Do they truly understand and demonstrate expertise in the converging macro-trends of millennials, multiculturalism, and women? What is the composition of your account team including the creative director?

3. Does your sales force know how to sell, prospect, and acquire new customers who are women? Can your sales force clearly articulate the female benefits of your companies' products to women?

Deepening Your Learning

— *Book* —

Why She Buys: The New Strategy for Reaching the World's Most Powerful Consumers, Bridget Brennan

— *Online Article* —

"The Female Economy," *Harvard Business Review* (Sep 2009)

— *Website* —

http://www.WomenKind.net

Chapter 5

The Field Factor

"Greatness is not a function of circumstance.
Greatness, it turns out, is largely a matter
of conscious choice, and discipline."

— Jim Collins, *Good to Great* [45]

"Congratulations, Jeff, you and your wife will be moving to Roanoke, Virginia."

I along with eleven other candidates had just completed the nine-month training program at The Coca-Cola Company. In exchange for a world-class training experience, a great job, and a company car, I had agreed to enter the Franchise Managers Training Program. The only stipulation was that upon graduation, I was required to accept the city to which I would be assigned.

The next stage in my career tour of duty would be in Roanoke. My other classmates received their assignments as well, to such exotic destinations as Eugene, Oregon; Beaumont, Texas; Birmingham, Alabama; and Corinth, Mississippi.

The Coca-Cola Company had already moved me nine months earlier to Minneapolis with my wife and new baby, and that move was preceded by a relocation to Green Bay, Wisconsin, by Procter & Gamble. Following two years in Roanoke, I would also spend time in Oklahoma City, Indianapolis, Chicago, and eventually Atlanta. Such was life in 1980s corporate America.

There were three brilliant women in my class of eleven. And over the course of the coming years, all three would end up leaving the company, done in by marriage and children, multiple relocations, challenging customers, bad bosses and a lack of sponsorship. Each exhibited incredible potential, yet within ten years of their first assignment, all had left the Coke system. While it's no longer 1985, I believe many of the circumstances then surrounding their "opting out" are pretty much the same challenges women are facing now.

The Key to Breaking the 16 Percent Barrier

Earlier I mentioned that women still only hold 16 percent of C-Suite roles. For this reason, this is probably the most important chapter in the book. If we are going to move more women into the C-Suite we must fix the broken pipeline that leads from the Field to the corner office. This subject is so important because the "Field Force" is who actually runs the company: sales generates revenue and operations is directly responsible for the profit and loss of the organization while supply chain and manufacturing routinely house the most significant costs borne by organization. And the Field is still controlled overwhelmingly by men.

To break the 16 Percent Barrier, it will take a ten- to fifteen-year commitment of advancing women in sales and operations to significantly change this number.

Why so long? That's the minimum number of years necessary to have the skill set to reach the Divisional President level. As of July 2014, there were twenty-four women CEOs in the Fortune 500. [46] This represents only 4.8 percent of the 500 and the following illustrates where they spent the majority of their careers. Even the women who spent the bulk of their careers in staff positions did not achieve the CEO title without having taken on an operations role for a period of time.

The Career Path of Women CEOs [47]

Name	Company	Majority of Career Role	Primarily Operations Background
Mary Barra	GM (#7)	Supply chain and engineering	Yes
Meg Whitman	HP (#17)	Consulting and operations at eBay	Yes
Virginia Rometty	IBM (#23)	Sales, marketing, and strategy	Yes
Patricia A. Woertz	Archer Daniels (#27)	Finance, strategic planning	Yes
Indra K. Nooyi	PepsiCo, Inc. (#43)	Finance, strategic planning	No
Marillyn Hewson	Lockheed Martin (#59)	Operations	Yes
Ellen J. Kullman	DuPont (#86)	Marketing and operations	Yes
Irene B. Rosenfeld	Mondelez (#89)	Marketing and operations	Yes
Phebe Novakovic	General Dynamics (#99)	Strategic planning and operations	Yes
Carol M. Meyrowitz	TJX (#108)	Merchandising and operations	Yes
Lynn J. Good	Duke Energy (#123)	Finance and operations	No
Ursula M. Burns	Xerox (#137)	Supply chain and operations	Yes
Deanna M. Mulligan	Guardian (#245	Consulting and operations	Yes
Kimberly Bowers	CST Brands (#266)	Mergers and acquisitions, law	No
Debra L. Reed	Sempra Energy (#267)	Engineering and finance	Yes
Barbara Rentler	Ross Stores (#277)	Merchandising	No
Sheri S. McCoy	Avon (#282)	R&D and operations	Yes
Denise M. Morrison	Campbell's Soup (#315)	Marketing, sales, and operations	Yes
Susan M. Cameron	Reynolds Amer. (#329)	Marketing, sales, and operations	Yes
Heather Bresch	Mylan (#377)19	Operations	Yes
Ilene Gordon	Ingredion (#412)	Supply chain and operations	Yes
Jacqueline Hinman	CH2M Hill (#437)	Consulting and operations	Yes
Kathleen M. Mazzarella	Graybar Electric (#449)	Strategic planning, sales, operations	Yes
Gracia C. Martore	Gannett (#481)	Finance and operations	No

The vast majority of these women come from STEM backgrounds and most have an MBA from a major business school. (Two notable women you may not see on the list at this time are Merissa Mayer, CEO of Yahoo!, which ranks 522 on the Fortune 1000 list and Sheryl Sandberg, Chief Operating Officer of Facebook. As of this writing, Facebook does not have a female CEO title in its organizational chart.)

So why are there so few women in the C-suite? Contrary to what many people believe, it's not a lack of ambition. Study upon study shows that women certainly don't lack ambition or desire. A recent global survey of 1,421 global executives by McKinsey & Company bears this out. [48]

W Eighty-three percent of men desire to reach a top management position.

W Eighty-two percent of women share the same desire.

"The survey results," says Sandrine Devillard, a director in McKinsey's Paris office, "show that female executives are ambitious and sure of their ability to succeed. There really is no difference between men and women. We were so flabbergasted by this because it's so counter to common wisdom."

The McKinsey study also found that more women (83 percent) than men (74 percent) said they have a strong desire to advance to the next level within their organizations.

Having the ambition, moxie, and a desire to ascend the corporate ladder is a given. Ambitious men and women then realize the real contest works through their own personal experiences with opportunities, landmines, good and bad managers, the resources to drive results, and a little luck along the way.

Truly understanding what and how leaders are grown in the field requires us to examine the challenges that exist on a daily basis in this part of the organization, some are obvious and some are never discussed.

These challenges are many and multi-faceted, and vary widely from organization to organization. I am choosing to highlight three areas that I believe may be some of the highest leverage points and greatest barriers to advancing women.

1. **The Field is TOUGH!** Not just for women, but for men as well. It's challenging for anyone to survive sales, supply chain, manufacturing, and operations, and the lifestyle that is required to be successful and thrive.

2. **Men and women assess talent differently.** Field managers often lack the ability to hire, develop, and advance people unlike themselves. This is partially a result of lack of training, but also an inability to differentiate men and women's strengths regarding leadership competencies.

3. **The realities of the Field.** Women are often faced, to a much greater degree, with the series of life choices and micro inequities that only women can experience—situations that are not always supported or accommodated by organizations, especially in the Field.

To truly break the C-suite barrier, organizations must examine all aspects of the challenges of the Field. Chapter 5 will examine what goes on "in the Field." Chapters 6 and 7 will build on these issues as the need for critical programs and processes are magnified in the field including the intersection of talent, meritocracies, sponsorship, and quite frankly—luck.

The Field is TOUGH!

The Field is a tough place to choose for building one's career. A life of sales can be fraught with challenging quotas and customers. Manufacturing and supply chain, historically dominated by men, have their own set of workplace challenges, and operations is often a sixty- to seventy-hour pressure cooker of a workweek. To advance in the company it is critical for leaders to have a wide breadth of experience.

This helps them examine different market challenges and think strategically. One of the most important ways to build a breath of experiences is take multiple assignments across a host of geographies.

The following story is based on real events from people in field roles. I have changed the names and the cities. If you talk to men and women in your organization who spent the bulk of their careers in field roles I have no doubt you will hear very similar stories multiple times.

Victor and Evelyn

Victor and Evelyn both graduated head of their class from a top business school and accepted high entry-level sales positions with a midsize Fortune 500 company. As in most organizations, two-thirds of the roles were in field sales, which Victor and Evelyn wholeheartedly accepted, along with eight other high potentials in that recruitment sweep.

Victor was sent to Raleigh, and Evelyn to Louisville. Both were rock stars and each was promoted within eighteen months—Victor to Charlotte and Evelyn to Cincinnati.

Eventually, they both met the love of their lives, and each got married. Another eighteen months later, both were asked to take significant multistate manager level jobs with significant travel and people responsibility. These promotions would send Victor to Miami and Evelyn to Detroit. Victor didn't hesitate at the chance, even though the woman he married had a budding, successful career in Charlotte.

Evelyn's husband was a bit more apprehensive. He was well entrenched in his career and was hesitant to uproot and look for work in a new city. However, realizing Evelyn's potential, he agreed to move. While both relocations were challenging, Victor's wife was more accepting and supportive, Evelyn's husband was reluctant, but also supportive. These micro-issues are one of the elements of the challenges of life in the Field.

Evelyn's husband was also concerned about the amount of travel that she would be doing and the impact that this would have on their lives and future family plans. Like most women, Evelyn would end up assuming most of the responsibility for the changes that would be occurring.

Victor and Evelyn were again achieving comparable, out-of-the-park results. However, the work was significantly more challenging. Victor's job was made a bit easier as he was working for Scott, another ascending star, who saw eye-to-eye with Victor on many issues.

Victor also had the opportunity to work closely with Mark. Mark was functionally higher then Victor and worked in another department, yet Mark took Victor under his wing. They developed a great friendship and would often grab a beer after work while Mark explained to Victor "how the company really works!"

As a result of Victor's relationship with Scott and getting great coaching from Mark, Victor was given multiple opportunities for special projects. In Scott's performance review of Victor he wrote,

> *"Victor's results are terrific. He is very capable, a sound strategic thinker . . . a real team player who's able to reach across departments to garner the resources within the company to be successful. A natural leader, Victor can quickly set a course of action and engage his team for results."*

Evelyn, on the other hand, had a bit more of a challenging situation. She was working for Ron, a career Field VP who never quite made it to the senior ranks. Evelyn and Ron didn't exactly see eye-to-eye on how to handle situations with her team. In Evelyn's performance review Ron's wrote,

> *"Evelyn is a solid performer who exceeds her targets. She can sometimes be challenging to work with. She tends to be argumentative and aggressive in meetings and asks too many questions. She has difficulty seeing the big picture and thinking strategically . . . she just needs to talk and act like a leader."*

Evelyn persevered and put up great numbers. Yet Ron didn't see leadership potential in her, and when opportunities for special projects arose, he didn't consider nominating or sponsoring her. Evelyn knew she was in a tough spot and reasoned if she just put her head down and worked harder, her performance would speak for itself.

She often passed on office social outings as she saw them as a waste of time. She was the only women of her level in the office and did not see any value in hanging out with a bunch of guys. "I have too much work, and need to be with my family at the end of the day. I don't have time for nonessential activities in my crazy, busy life."

The Field is tough: multiple relocations, pressure to perform, challenging management, and trying to have some semblance of a normal life. We'll return to this typical story of organizational life later in the chapter. For now, let's take a deeper dive into the realities that both Victor and Evelyn are facing and why the role of effectively training leaders becomes critical to the field really owning and developing talent.

Men and Women Assess Talent Differently

Attracting, retaining, and developing talent are often considered HR responsibilities. I believe talent is a responsibility of all leaders, especially those in the Field. If the Field is the path to moving more women into senior leadership roles, then we need to hold line managers responsible for the retention, advancement, and development of their key female talent.

> *The challenge is that men and women assess leadership competencies quite differently.*

In Catalyst's report, *Women "Take Care," Men "Take Charge,"* 296 senior business leaders were asked to rate men and women's skills across common leadership behaviors. [49] They were not asked "who's better," but only to rate each gender's effectiveness in each of the behaviors. When the results were compiled as to what men and women said about each other, the findings became quite revealing.

Gender Bias in the Perception of Women's Leadership Behaviors

Competency	Men Replies		Women Replies		Opportunity/Issue
	Men ≥ Women	Women > Men	Men ≥ Women	Women > Men	
Team Building	=			x	
Mentoring	=			x	
Consulting	=			x	
Networking	=		x		Possible Development Area for Women
Supporting		x		x	
Rewarding		x		x	
Problem Solving	x			x	Possible Area of Gender Bias
Inspiring	x			x	Possible Area of Gender Bias

The bottom line of the study shows that,

- Men rated themselves and women as equally skilled in Teambuilding, Mentoring, and Consulting, while in all three areas, women scored themselves higher than men.

- In Networking, men rated themselves and women as being equally skilled while women rated men at being better at it.

- In Supporting and Rewarding, men ranked women higher as did women.

This reveals a major difference in how men and women define and demonstrate that competency, and how they expect and perceive it in the other gender.

The last column to the chart—Opportunity/Issue—is added to comment on those areas where the rating by men and women revealed differences and I believe are areas of potential bias for men and women or may be possible developmental opportunities for women.

This disparity in assessing leadership competencies clearly speaks to the series of questions I asked you in Chapter 3 when considering your talent. Once your organization has internalized the business case, you must then look at what has to change. I believe that leaders need to do a significantly better job in understanding and leveraging male and female differences in the workplace, and this study on gender bias in the perception of leadership can provide those areas of discussion.

Let's take a deeper dive into those three areas that show inconsistencies in the perceptions of men and women, specifically:

- Networking
- Problem Solving
- Inspiring

Networking as a Sign of Leadership

On the surface, networking should be an absolute no-brainer for women. Their networks are typically ten times the size of their male colleagues! Catalyst Research defines Networking as . . .

> *Developing and maintaining relationships with others who may provide information or support.*

What we start to see in this definition is not just having a lot of people in your network. It's about effectively utilizing those contacts for information or support. Given this definition, men may in fact be better at this competency. Most men in organizations, when faced with an issue or challenge, do not hesitate to pick up the phone and "call in a favor from a colleague."

In *The Sponsor Effect: Breaking through the Last Glass Ceiling,* Sylvia Hewlett clearly distinguishes the different reasons women and men network, especially in a business environment. [50]

**"*Women tend to network for relationships, while men network to compete and win.*
Asking for favors and returning favors are just part of the unwritten male code."**

In fact, it's not something men even discuss a lot. When men meet other men, we immediately shake hands, give our job title, and describe what we do, or ask, "What do you do?" We expect the men we meet to do the same. We rarely examine whether it's right or wrong, we just think of how we can best network with other men for business connections. We're pretty much all thinking the same way, all the time.

This fascinating topic always surfaces in my workshops with women. Most of the women I know would not hesitate for a minute to help or do a favor for a friend or colleague. Yet they are incredibly hesitant to pick up the phone and ask someone in their vast network for help or a strategic connection for themselves. The responses I typically get from women range from, "It just doesn't feel comfortable" to "I don't want to jeopardize our friendship."

Seeking out and gathering information and resources is actually a significant part of being a leader. In our story above, this was something that Scott saw Victor exercise repeatedly and in fact valued it as a demonstration of leadership.

Sylvia Hewlett goes on to address the effect of women's reluctance to work their network.

"*Women's aversion to this kind of naked quid pro quo translates into a wealth of supportive peers, but a dearth of unused relationship capital.*"

Women view initiating and developing relationships for self-advancing purposes as an uncomfortable but necessary evil. They tend not to engage in the practice of seeking out and cultivating relationships with powerful people for self-benefit as men do. They don't see it as a demonstration of leadership.

In Hewlett's, *The Sponsorship Effect*, Rosalind Hudnell, Vice President and Chief Diversity Officer at Intel, shares her observation on the way men network:

> *"I think you'll find women generally network for social purposes, whereas men network to compete and win. If a man is sitting next to a senior executive, he'll see it as an opportunity to connect with someone who one day might help him win; so he'll deliberately attempt to build that relationship and take advantage of that opportunity. He may even go about it in the most obnoxious way, but at least he'll ask and make the attempt to connect."*

Problem Solving for the Best Solution

It's interesting how teams can come together, look at the exact same data, and draw completely different conclusions. The inability of getting teams to work effectively together and communicate openly may be the biggest detriment to organizational effectiveness and profitability. And it's one of those areas that men and women approach quite differently. Interestingly, the difference begins to show itself at the very onset in how each gender approaches an issue.

Men approach problem solving by narrowing the field of options and focusing in on the fastest solution.

Women approach problem solving by expanding the field of options and exploring for the best solution.

Unending discoveries in brain physiology and hormonal chemistry are pointing us to a direction that men and women approach problem solving in equally valuable, but very different manners. To men, problem solving tends to be either a left- or right-brain activity.

Like a tunnel to their intentions, sequential thinking allows men to concentrate and converge more fully on a limited number of solutions.

In problem-solving mode men's neurons connect faster, but in a linear fashion as shown in the diagram below. Women tend to solve problems using their right- and left-brain simultaneously, with connections moving back and forth across the brain faster and in an interconnected fashion.

This allows women to be more holistic and contextual in their thinking and as a result, generate more possible solutions.

This diagram of the brain activity of females and males shows how the sexes engage both hemispheres of their brain. [51] What does this look like in real life though? Consider how this plays out in meetings. Men, at the onset of a discussion, will often immediately offer up a solution. Feeling confident and with their testosterone flowing, they will then defend their solution to the death. Women, actually seeking to obtain the right answer, will offer up multiple options and ask for questions, seeking input from everyone on the team.

While she may view this as constructive, the men in the room tend to see it as being indecisive and not having a firm point of view.

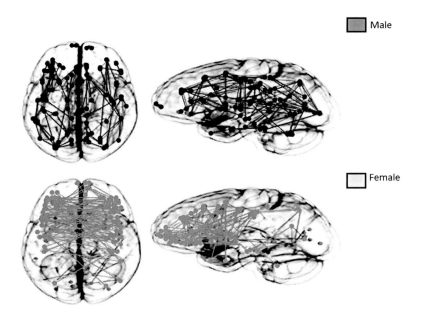

Male

Female

University of Pennsylvania [52]

If men view problem solving as an opportunity to be quick and decisive, rather than an exercise in exploring multiple options to get to the right answer, they may question a woman's analytical ability and confidence in making a decision.

Compounding this issue is that there is a likelihood that she may have not been heard in past meetings nor had her ideas validated. A woman's natural reaction then is to ask more questions and seek more data to confirm her point of view, which her male colleagues may also view as lacking self-confidence and decisiveness.

Is what I've just described overly simplistic and rife with generalizations? The answer is yes . . . and no. I know many women who are brilliant problem solvers and quite decisive; and I know many men who are outstanding at seeking out other points of views to validate their own. This is why I list problem solving as an area of *possible* bias for men.

Does your organization look for decisiveness from the loudest voices in the room, or do you value instead finding the best possible solution?

I challenge you to observe the difference between decisiveness and effective problem solving and ask that you try this on for yourself in your next meeting.

To stress further the importance of this topic, if you are a senior field leader who is charged with assessing talent for promotional opportunities and special projects, do you understand the subtle differences in how problem solving may play itself out on your teams? As we witnessed earlier in our story, Evelyn and her boss, Ron, didn't see eye-to-eye when it came to solving issues.

Do you actively seek out different opinions and genuinely understand and embrace the differences on your team, or do you see them as challenging and contradictory to the status quo?

Inspiring Greatness in Others

We often think of leaders as dominant and ambitious—as embodying qualities that, in our culture, closely match the behavior of men. On the other hand, the traits that often define women's leadership such as inclusiveness, empathy, and sharing are seen as less vital to leadership. It can often result in women being evaluated less positively than men for those critical, front line positions.

A recent Catalyst study explores the differences in how men and women lead and why organizations need to "check this powerful bias" so as not to underutilize any segment of their talent pool. This study reveals how women and men define their leadership role and how cultural influences are preventing men (and some women) from recognizing the value in the way women lead. [53]

When men and women describe their leadership and how they inspire those with whom they work, the men are more likely to characterize their style as *transactional*, though they don't use that exact word. They speak of their ability to inspire as a series of transactions with subordinates—exchanging rewards for services rendered or punishment for inadequate performance.

Men often adhere to a command and control style of leadership with minimal personal interaction with peers and subordinates. Men tend to give as they expect to receive and for the same reason tend to avoid conflict at work and give others space to solve their own issues.

Women, on the other hand, are more likely to describe themselves in ways that characterize their style of leadership as *transformational—*

getting subordinates to alter their own self-interests into the interest of the group through a concern for a broader goal. Women express their leadership thorough personal characteristics like interpersonal skills, hard work, and personal connections rather than through their own organizational stature and power.

Women actively work to make their interactions with subordinates positive for everyone involved. All these things reflect their belief that inspiring employees to contribute and to feel powerful and important is a win-win outcome—good for the employees and the organization.

You'll often hear women say,

"Encouraging participation, inspiring others, and enhancing self-worth gets others excited about their work."

It's interesting though how men and women both consider themselves stronger than the other in inspiring others. It makes this a difficult impasse for women who want to be authentic in their own style of leadership and confident in their approach to inspiring greatness in others. While women see this orientation as an important aspect of leadership for the good of the organization, men, and some women, tend to view it as not taking charge and leading and inspiring others.

The male model of business is the dominant model, especially in the Field, and this model has defined leadership competencies on the front lines for generations. It's the dominant model from which leadership traits are most often drawn, practiced, and promoted.

The challenging part is this often represents a "double bind dilemma" for women. [54]

If "corporate behavioral norms" were placed on a continuum from hard to soft, men would have a significantly wider acceptable behavior range than women. We have all witnessed this in our corporate lives. Most men can be seen as ultra-aggressive and will be labeled as great leaders. Women, on the other hand, will be labeled a word that rhymes with "witch."

After having heard from literally hundreds of businesswomen in conferences and workshops and from many businessmen that I've worked with over the years, I have created this visualization to represent and compare the "acceptable ranges of behaviors" between men and women.

A Double Bind Dilemma

Acceptable Range for Men

Acceptable Range for Women

Corporate Behavioral Norms

ULTRA AGGRESSIVE

behavior is loud, physically animated and can be characterized by the use of profanity.

Midpoint

OVERLY PASSIVE

behavior is non-confrontational, quiet and characterized by Shrinking or pulling back.

This dilemma conspires to put women into the untenable situation of the "Goldilocks Effect." Female leaders are often seen as too soft or too hard but never "just right."

Do this own exercise in your company. Watch and observe acceptable ranges of behaviors. I think you will see first-hand that the range of "acceptable corporate behaviors" women are allowed to exhibit is significantly narrower than men.

So far I've examined the challenges of being in the Field: multiple relocations, tough work, and how gender bias may show up in assessing talent environments. Before we can leave any discussion regarding the Field there are two other realities that we need to examine.

The Realities of the Field

Let's return to our story.

As it happens in the course of career and life, both Victor and Evelyn started a family.

When Victor's daughter was born, it was decided that Victor's wife would stay home and take care of their new daughter. Even though she had reestablished her career in Miami, she decided to step off the career train for a few years, as it was just plain easier for the family. Given Victor's travel schedule it would just be easier to have one parent stay at –home. When Victor took a whole week off to spend with his newborn daughter, everyone at the office measured him as being a good father and caring husband.

When Evelyn gave birth, she took sixteen weeks off starting in the middle of September to be with her newborn son. At the end of those four months, Evelyn returned to work and found her life a whole lot more complicated.

Being a resourceful, hardworking person, she cobbled together a nanny, day care, and other support systems for their newborn son, and found a way to balance the demands of her work with her personal life. Evelyn's husband continued to work full-time as well. While the two incomes helped with the additional expenses, it added significantly more stress to both their lives but especially hers. She would often spend extra time having to plan and make a coverage plans for her child as she traveled on a weekly basis.

A few years later, Victor and Evelyn would both have a second child and upon returning to work after a second sixteen weeks off, Evelyn struggled even harder to find that balance again.

One topic that is rarely discussed in companies is the real challenges faced by women (and men) when children arrive.

Is There a Baby Penalty?

Answering that specific question is not the intent of this book. My point is that if you want to win with women, you have to have honest dialogue. I have spoken to hundreds of women in researching this book. When I ask them about this topic they will tell you, "It's a baby reality." There are many sides to this debate.

I have heard senior female leaders express that companies need to work harder to ensure that inequities do not exist and that women do not deserve to be leapfrogged as a result of time off. I have also heard from other senior female leaders who acknowledge that business has to continue. Organizations today simply do not have the time or capacity to wait while a woman is on maternity leave. Customers still need to be served and business still needs to be transacted, it's just a reality of work today. One woman speaking confidentially to me put it this way,

> *"It's a combination of joy and guilt. While you want to rejoice in this miracle, in the back of your mind, you're feeling guilty because others are having to pick up your share of the work. To make matters worse, there are some bosses who just don't get it. I worked for one guy who clearly didn't understand. When I returned from maternity leave with my first child, I remember him saying, 'Well, that's sixteen weeks you owe me.' I was so outraged! I said nothing but immediately put my resume on the street."*

My goal is to point out the realities and to create conversations in organizations and the baby penalty is obviously one of those.

One comment I often receive when I tell the Victor and Evelyn story during my workshops is the "free-pass" that men get in the story. Merely saying Victor's wife chose to "stay home" is really letting men off the hook from a family responsibility standpoint. As I mentioned, this is based on a true story and I have heard similar stories repeated dozens of times.

It does bring up a very interesting dynamic that is still taking place in American households on a daily basis for working couples. [55]

W   Forty-nine percent of women do housework–such as cleaning or doing laundry compared to 19 percent of men.

W   Sixty-eight percent of women compared with 42 percent of men do food preparation or cleanup.

W   Among adults living in households with children under age 6, women spent one hour providing physical care (such as bathing or feeding a child) to household children; by contrast, men spent 26 minutes providing physical care.

Even in dual income households where women out-earn men, they are still more likely to assume more childcare, cooking, cleaning, and laundry responsibilities than men are. [56]

Most women, particularly those with children, will readily acknowledge when they leave work, they go home to their second full-time job. It should be noted, the same report stated that men today are in fact doing more household/childcare work than ever before in history, however, it is far from a parity situation with women.

Carol Evan's CEO and President of *Working Mother* Magazine says one of the biggest challenges is that senior leadership today still thinks it's the 1960s. [57]

"One element that is stalling progress is still an unconscious bias with many male leaders today. This is because most male leaders today were raised in a household by a working father and stay-at-home mother. As they themselves progressed in organizations they replicated this model. Even in 2015 it is hard for senior leaderships not be guided by these 1960 principles that absolutely no longer apply. That is not reality today. In most households today, both parents work outside the household and there is no one size fits all

lifestyle. For companies to complete and win they must change and adapt to the new reality today."

There are some powerful shifts that have taken place over the past few decades that are impacting family dynamics in a big way today: [58]

W In 40 percent of U.S. households, a mother is either the sole or primary earner for her family.

W Twenty-four percent of households include a wife who earns more than her husband does. This number was 6 percent in 1960.

W In 2007, before the recession, 20 percent of women considered full-time work a more ideal situation than part-time work. In 2012, that percent increased to 32 percent.

W Just 28 percent of Americans agree that it's better for a marriage if the husband earns more than the wife.

W As of 2011, there are more married-couple families with children (23 percent) in which the wife is more educated than the husband.

There is no one-size-fits-all solution. Change will come from dialogue and as leaders we need to be prepared for the conversations. This is not an issue solely regulated to the field as all levels of the organizations are impacted by this dilemma.

Frustration in organizations is reaching a tipping point. A close colleague of mine with an MBA from a world-class school and thriving career at a Fortune 100 company is now a stay-at-home mom. She summed up her thoughts on the entire subject,

"There is huge problem women have when trying to balance raising children and at the same time occupying a seat in executive management. If a women is an executive with children—rare, since most of the women in senior leadership at my company did not have children—she either had a stay-at-home-husband, a relative living with them, or a live-in au pair or nanny.

"When you are making that kind of money, it is not a problem. But what about women who aren't making the kind of money to support all that help, or don't have a husband who completely puts his career aside - or on hold? It is hard to GET to executive management if you can't put in the same kind of hours as your male colleague. The patriarchal corporate structure will have to collapse upon itself and re-build from the ground up before it is truly a working mom-friendly atmosphere!"

How would the women in your company answer the question, "Do you think there is a baby penalty at our company?"

In this chapter, we've have looked into many of the challenges found in "the Field," a difficult but critical place for organizations to examine to fix your companies female talent pipeline. We have examined the competencies that are important to leaders and revealed the different ways men and women view and exercise these traits. Finally, I raised challenging questions regarding the baby penalty, and changing family/household dynamics that organizations need to begin to have dialogue around if they are to advance women in all levels including the C-suite.

The organizational processes and programs that will help us in these areas will be the focus of our next chapter.

Summary Points from Chapter 5

- The Field is so important because the "Field Force" is who actually runs the company: sales generates revenue and operations is directly responsible for the profit and loss of the organization while supply chain and manufacturing routinely house the most significant costs borne by organization. And the Field is still controlled overwhelmingly by men.

- The Field is the pipeline to the C-suite. Today women only occupy about 16 percent of C-suite jobs with the majority of them being staff functions. If we truly want to break the 16 percent barrier, it will take a ten- to fifteen-year commitment of advancing women in sales and operations to significantly change this number.

- Field managers and leaders often lack the ability to understand and advance people unlike themselves. This is not necessarily a result of training, but an inability to differentiate men's and women's strengths and leadership competencies.

- Men and women have significantly different viewpoints regarding the competencies of Networking, Problem Solving, and Inspiring.

- Women are often faced, to a much greater degree, with the series of life choices that only women can experience— situations that are not always supported or accommodated by organizations.

- Organizations must be prepared to talk about the new realities facing all workers and families as it is reaching a tipping point in organizations.

WHY WOMEN Readiness Assessment

1. What does your talent pipeline for women look like in the Field? What are the challenges and barriers that you can identify and do you have a plan to address them?

2. As you examine the leadership competency model for your company how are you developing leaders to evaluate talent that doesn't think, look, and act like they do?

3. Is your leadership prepared to tackle real-life issues that impact all talent and are present in organizations today such as The Baby Penalty and new models of work/life responsibilities?

Deepening Your Learning

— *Book* —

Through the Labyrinth: The Truth About How Women Become Leaders, Alice H. Eagly, Linda L. Carli

— *Online Article* —

"Women '"Take Care," Men "Take Charge": Stereotyping of U.S. Business Leaders Exposed," Catalyst Research (2005)

— *Website* —

http://www.WorkingMother.com

Chapter 6

The HR Paradox

"The biggest men and women with the biggest ideas can be shot down by the smallest men and women."

—Cheryl Conner,
The 10 Paradoxical Commandments of Business [59]

"I'm sorry, we're going to have to let you go."

How many times have you heard that message? Business results were not up to par and a new CEO was brought in to shake things up. Today this seems commonplace, though it was very much not the norm just fifteen years ago.

The year was 2000, and The Coca-Cola Company was undergoing its first major layoff. Business results were not up to par and a new CEO was brought in. Two things would happen of note in 1999: the first was the laying off of almost 6,000 employees across the system; the second was a settlement of an almost $200 million discrimination lawsuit. [60]

As I mentioned in Chapter 1, I would witness my own role change from running franchise training to moving into diversity education. On one hand, we were letting thousands of incredibly talented people leave the company. At the same time, Coca-Cola, in many regards, was undergoing a watershed moment in order to become a much better employer for all employees. In my mind, a truly a greater paradox could not be imagined—and it is just as true today in many organizations.

Let me explain why I see this as a paradox.

What may seem like sound reasoning on the part of companies to become better and financially stronger places in the short term is entirely counter to the statement often made by those very same companies, "People are our greatest asset."

Leaders and organizations say they need great talent, yet every day, amazing people leave companies as the result of what seems like an ongoing series of reorganizations and restructures. Many others leave on their own accord by refusing to work for bad managers. Regardless of the situation, there are unintended consequences that come from cutting into your talent muscle and asking good people to leave. This paradox is especially true for female talent. It is often unknown and unintended consequences that force women to leave their companies.

There are literally dozens of HR Programs and Processes that are necessary to create a world-class culture. My focus is to examine a few key areas that are standard practices in most companies, but with a lens of the role they play in operationalizing your Integrated Women's

Leadership Strategy. I want to highlight these areas to help non-HR leaders understand that for companies to truly to get talent right, these programs and processes must be understood and executed by all leaders and managers in the organization.

Additionally I want to support and challenge HR professionals to raise their game. There has never been a more critical time for you to gain your rightful seat at the leadership table and lead this dialogue for your organization.

I will examine three broad areas highlighting the necessary programs and processes needed to make be successful today with women. Specifically I will examine,

1. Recruitment - the key critical elements needed to bring more women into your company.
2. Retention - the programs and processes needed to keep your highly talented women.
3. Advancement - the solutions and barriers that are prohibiting organizations from advancing women to the senior ranks of your company.

The outcome of this chapter is to help leaders and managers understand that within each of these elements a challenging paradox potentially exists. I want to identify this paradox and provide dialogue points to help you to engage in this conversation in your organization. Each is critical to not just attracting, developing, and retaining women but to building a best–in-class organization.

Finally, the solutions that follow are best practices of leading organizations. As much of this is sensitive data, I cannot list the names of the organizations, but I can attest that these are, in fact, best practices that are being used and implemented within the Fortune 500.

Recruitment

I use the word "recruitment" to encompass a host of elements including sourcing, selection, and executing an initial hire. For our focus on women I want to highlight two key Paradoxes that are being examined in a new light in leading companies: Selection and Compensation.

The Selection Paradox—Non-Biased Hiring

Sourcing today has taken on a new level of sophistication. Every organization is utilizing online tools, campus recruiting, and other internal and external hiring initiatives. One of the great challenges is finding the available talent that fits the needs of the organization while maintaining their focus on a diverse sourcing pool of candidates.

As noted before, we are approaching 85 percent of new entries into the workforce being women and minorities. One of the significant challenges I often hear is the need to have diverse candidate pools and if that is a legal process. For now, I'm going to hold off the discussion of diverse talent and quotas until Chapter 8 when I explore it within the context of scorecards and metrics. For most leading-edge companies today, the requirements of diverse candidate pools are a given.

While organizations are broadening their pools, new research is showing that many companies are actually being short-circuited by the language used in job descriptions and company profiles. A recent study commissioned by the American Psychological Association, reveals that gender bias in the wording of job postings does exist and tends to perpetuate gender inequality. [61]

> *Highly masculine wording used in the job posting reduces women's appeal because it signals that women may not fit in or belong.*

The APA used engineering job descriptions in their study but the lessons from this example are applicable to any industry, company, or position.

Male-themed words (italicized) used in an engineering job description:

Company Description

We are a *dominant* engineering firm that *boasts* many *leading* clients. We are *determined* to *stand apart* from the *competition*.

Qualifications

Strong communication and *influencing* skills. Ability to *perform individually* in a *competitive* environment. *Superior* ability to *satisfy* customers and manage company's association with them.

Responsibilities

Direct project groups to *manage* project *progress* and ensure accurate task *control*. *Determine compliance* with client's *objectives*.

Non-biased words used in an engineering job description:

Company Description

We are a *community* of engineers who have effective *relationships* with many *satisfied* clients. We are *committed* to *understanding* the engineering sector *intimately*.

Qualifications

Proficient oral and written communications skills. Collaborates well in a *team* environment. *Sensitive* to clients' needs, can *develop warm* client *relationships*.

Responsibilities

Provide general support to project team in a manner *complimentary* to the company. *Help* clients with construction activities.

Research shows that women job seekers were "more interested in male-dominated jobs when advertisements were unbiased." In this way, qualified female applicants, and many male candidates for that matter, are opting out of jobs in which they could have otherwise performed well.

Having sourced candidates, we can now examine the hiring process. Again, the interviewing process is filled with significant challenges of bias, be they men or women. Many hiring managers often have a pre-conceived notation of what they're looking for—someone who fits their definition of leadership, which is most often based on a traditional male model of leadership.

The result?

- They assess candidates through a male-oriented paradigm.
- They view women who don't reflect that model as lacking potential or harboring self-doubt.
- They view women who are behaving like men as overly aggressive.

As previously mentioned, many best-in-class companies ensure that they have diverse candidate pools. Of equal or greater importance is the need for a diverse interview panel. Bringing multiple points of view of gender, culture, and organizational background helps provide a grounded and balanced approach. This also serves a dual purpose: one, to help ensure a fair, unbiased discussion; and two, the candidate can see and interact with someone who is similar to them. This sends a significant message to your future employee that this is a welcoming environment for them.

The Compensation Paradox: Fair but not Equitable

We have all heard and read about the wage gap between men and women. Arguments have been made on both sides that women tend to migrate into lower paying jobs compared to their male peers. My point is not to debate wage equity in the broader marketplace but to take a deeper examination of what's going on in your company. Are your pay policies in fact fair *AND* equitable to women? Even in organizations that have well-defined job grades and salary bands, women still tend to be paid, on average, less than men, and this statistic is static and unchanging.

> *For the last decade, median earnings for women working full time, year-round have been just 77 percent of men's earnings.* [62]

Additionally, women fall further and further behind over time. The American Association of University Women's research report *The Simple Truth about the Gender Pay Gap* found that women are paid about 90 percent of what men are paid until age thirty-five, when women's median earnings typically drop to 75–80 percent to that of men's. [63]

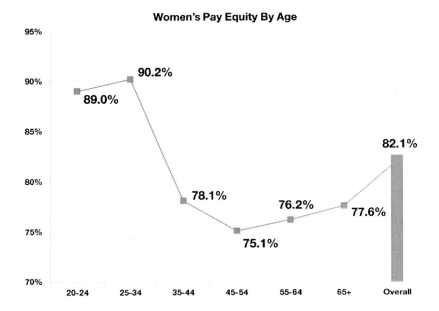

Women's Pay Equity By Age

Catalyst [64]

A major portion of the wage gap for women simply starts out when they leave college and join their first company. Research has shown very clearly that women do not negotiate their entry-level salary as fervently as their male classmates do. This is brought on by a couple of different reasons.

Let's look at an example that we know happens all the time. Rob and Janice are coming out of college with equal credentials. There's a high entry level management job that they both interview for at the same company. They know the job pays roughly in the $70,000 range. When Janice is asked her salary requirements, she says $68,000 to $72,000. Rob asks for $78,000 to $82,000.

As savvy businesspeople, we would make an offer to both of them. We would offer Janice $70,000 and Rob $80,000, and chances are both would accept it. This happens in large part because women are just much less likely to negotiate salary and make demands upfront.

Is this both fair and equitable? As a business person, if I can get someone $10,000 cheaper who has a comparable skill set, does that just not make good business sense?

The answer is that it's certainly fair, but is it equitable?

In her book, *Women Don't Ask: The High Cost of Avoiding Negotiation— And Positive Strategies for Change*, Linda Babcock found that male graduate students started at about a 7 percent higher salary than female graduates—a pay gap that worked out to about $4,000 a year. [65]

Digging deeper, Babcock and her researchers discovered why:

Only 7 percent of female students had negotiated their starting salaries.

In contrast, 57 percent of men had asked for more than initially offered.

This pay equity is then compounded by the subjective performance management system detailed above which would potentially give Rob 4 percent raises and Janice 3 percent raises, and over ten years this represents a significant gap that will exist for their entire careers.

Best-in-class companies are being proactive and taking a much more equitable approach. Revisiting the above scenario with the proactive mindset, at these top firms the hiring company would offer both Janice and Rob a starting salary of $75,000. The hiring company would obviously get Janice; she would be elated! But we could run the risk of losing Rob. The solution for best-in-class companies using this formula is to offer Rob a one-time bonus to bring him on board. While we've still initially paid Rob more to get him in the door, he is clearly starting at the same baseline level as Janice.

Is your organization both fair and equitable when making job offers?

Are you aware of an entry-level woman's hesitancy to negotiate salary?

Retention

There are litanies of programs that influence retention of talent. Engagement and the drivers of engagement were discussed in Chapters 2 and 3. Challenges to retention, specifically in the Field were addressed in Chapter 5. There are a number of other organizational and personal barriers that will be discussed later in the book. For now I want to highlight three areas that are typically hosted by and led by Human Resources, specifically, Performance Management, Learning and Development, and Employee Resource Groups.

The Performance Management Paradox: Subjectivity

"It's all about results!" This is the common theme that most organizations take when discussing performance management.

However, progressive companies today are not just looking at results but also evaluating people and managers on "how" those of results are obtained. Yet in almost every performance management discussion, subjectivity remains a critical concern. A person's natural tendency is to like, support, and advance people like themselves.

Ask yourself this question: Over the course of your career, how many hours of training did you receive to understand different approaches to problem solving, communications, and obtaining results? Chances are the ability to assess and value talent that is unlike "you" is a rarely taught and developed skill.

I know that in my years as a people manager, my consistent benchmark was to rate people just like me—as high performers. I acknowledge that this is my bias, however I believe this tendency exists in many managers today. Let's go back to the story of Victor and Evelyn to see how this plays out.

> *As a result of Victor's relationship with Scott and great coaching from Mark, Victor was given multiple opportunities for special projects. Scott saw Victor as a strategic thinker and real team player who was very capable and was able to garner resources within the company to be successful.*
>
> *Evelyn, on the other hand, was seen by her boss Ron as argumentative and posing too many questions in meetings. He saw her as taking on all of the work and had difficulty in delegating. He felt Evelyn just needed to think and act like a leader.*

***Both leaders were looking for the skills
and talents in their subordinates that they
were familiar with — that they saw in themselves.***

As I mentioned earlier results and performance are important, however *how* you obtain those results are also important. When the time comes for you to consider your "best of the best," what are those difference makers that separate your highest-rating employees from your "good" but not "great?" Are those differences truly objective or are they subjective?

Consider a few keywords that show up in our example above that are used in the assessment of virtually every rising leader. Subjective words like "strategic thinker," "a real team player," and "think and act like a leader." Are men more likely to rate other men higher? When it comes to the subjective nature of performance management, we would like to think that all managers are gender-blind and color-blind. Unfortunately, this is oftentimes not the case. We know the tendency is to evaluate subjective words on our individual reality.

Progressive organizations today are actually auditing performance ratings for consistency and fairness. Many organizations are finding that when they compile and cut performance ratings by gender and race, it is often the case that women and minorities are rated lower than that of their male peers. It should be noted that these progressive companies don't show systemic discrimination issues.

What you'll find when you peel back the onion is an inconsistency to see this trend across the organization, simply because of the dynamics of large numbers. Often the differences are very small. I would challenge you to ask this question of your company, the answer to which may surprise you.

> ## *"Does our organization have a calibration and review process for the way gender and race are equitably rated in our performance management process?"*

Finally, as a portion of that process, do you have a formal system for managers to get together and calibrate what successful performance looks like? We all know managers who never give a top rating to anyone in order to challenge everyone, or the manager who is overly positive about all their people and fights to ensure that everyone receives higher than average ratings. Both managers are well intended, but what is missing is a polished lens of fairness and equity. Companies today must allow managers to discuss and determine as a group what effective performance consistently looks like.

The Learning and Development Paradox - Culture Change vs. "Check the Box Activity"

Effective learning and development programs are critical elements yet unfortunately, most are just given a lukewarm reception in a solid diversity education plan. We all have images of what comes to mind when we're told were going to "diversity training." Too often, the training focuses on compliance rather than inspiring a frank dialogue about our differences and tying those differences to the bottom line.

Regarding gender, progressive companies are moving to change this by implementing learning annexes and workshops designed to improve gender awareness and improve the innovativeness and productivity of leaders and managers alike. Today, even discussing something as simple as gender is seen as a contentious discussion as opposed to an opportunity to learn.

How powerful is this? Do this exercise at the beginning of your next meeting by just asking a simple question: "When I say the word 'gender' within a work context, what words pop into your head?" Initially you will get the obligatory "men and women, boss/subordinate, colleague, friend, etc." After a few minutes you will start to hear words deeper words like, "sexism, double standards, don't listen, talk too much, bossy, condescending." You will get the point very quickly.

Are the words men and women use in your organization to describe each other positive or negative? Are these the words of a successful team?

Rather than minimizing and not talking about differences, programs have been developed to seek and understand the value of thinking differently when it comes to problem solving, decision making, leading teams, and achieving bottom line results. It is only through genuinely trying to understand the challenges and situations that women face that we can, not just as men but as leaders, be more successful in today's organizations.

My program, *The Evolved Leader, Men and Women Working Together for Team Success,* explores this topic on a very deep level and is one of the most successful initiatives my company runs. This workshop is designed to present the business case and economic value of gender diversity. Scientific research is presented to show men and women that nature, in addition to family upbringing, education, and culture, inform and influence how men and women think and act.

Different perspectives are allowed to surface in order to be probed and questioned. As a result, these processes and exercises lead to increased awareness of all participants of both genders.

This new mindset of men and women bringing their strengths and talking about their differences can absolutely be game changing when it comes to being more effective and efficient in our communications, problem solving, and decision making.

The Business Resource Groups Paradox: Wine and Whine vs. Business Enabler

Business Resource Groups (BRGs) refers to any number of organizational groups—from affinity groups to employee resource groups. Typically more prominent in larger organizations, these are groups that encompass many different demographics and are often guided by a formal governance process. As an example, many organizations today will have versions of women, minorities, LGBT, and veteran resource groups. You may also find new employee groups, millennial groups, groups for new parents, for people with disabilities, and a host of others.

BRGs can serve as powerful retention tools to allow cohort groups to network, share opportunities and challenges that they are facing, and allow people to feel more connected to the organization. BRGs, when given the proper structure and governance, can become invaluable tools for successful engagement. Too often though, organizations view the activities of these groups as merely opportunities for social or networking activities. One female business leader I know calls them "wine and whine sessions."

I also heard another male leader actually say,

"Why would we want THOSE people to get together and talk? Nothing good can obviously come out of it."

Apparently he doesn't think that groups of like-minded people actually get together to discuss and serve up ideas to make their department or organization stronger. Effectively constructed and tasked with strategic purpose, BRGs could become your pulse on the business in both the workplace and marketplace.

Do you really want to know what women think about working for the company? Just ask the members of their Business Resource Group.

Conduct pulse surveys and focus groups with your BRGs. And as with any other element of the business, hold your BRGs accountable to delivering value to the business. More importantly, your BRGs can serve to deepen the cultural competency of that specific group within the broader workforce population.

My first work in deepening my cultural competency regarding women actually started with a BRG. As I was assuming my role in diversity education, Coca-Cola was just starting to form Business Resource Groups. And as the "new diversity guy," I went to the kickoff events for all of the groups. When I got up to leave the first meeting of the women's group, the resource group's president approached me and asked, "Where are you going?"

I said that this first session was a membership drive for the women's group, it was something I wholeheartedly supported, but as a man, I would certainly not be expected to join!

Mary, the president of the Women's BRG, became quite indignant. "We need your help. In fact, I want you to lead the strategic planning process for the Coke women's business resource group."

Mary was not a woman who would take no for an answer and so . . .

I became the first male member of the Women's Business Resource Group. In hindsight, I will tell you this was a life-changing experience.

Not only did it deepen my cultural competency, it also increased my network within the company by about 200 people. Within six months, literally every senior woman in the company knew who I was and that I was their ally. I could never have brought this kind of positive exposure to my own brand without having joined that women's BRG.

For you men out there, I'm not suggesting that you join a BRG to be self-serving and build your own network but I will tell you though that being involved in any BRG is both personally fulfilling and tremendously beneficial to your career. There's no greater way to find out what's going on with people, truly spend time with them, and immerse yourself into their daily lives.

Advancement

The Women's Leadership Development Paradox: Fix the Women versus Fix the Culture (and the Men)

Each year, I attend a number of women's conferences and leadership events. They are filled with learning curriculum development areas and steps to get ahead in organizations. These conferences provide valuable opportunities for individualized learning assessment feedback, developing robust career paths, and extending and enhancing a woman's network. The issue I have is that many unintentionally seem to focus on the need to "fix women." This reinforces a woman's belief that if she builds one more skill or enhances one more competency, she will finally be ready for that next job.

I will acknowledge that these programs provide amazing insight and growth potentials. However, by reinforcing the need that skill development alone will advance their careers influences women into believing they are not ready when in fact they are.

A more powerful idea is highlighted by Rebecca Shambaugh in her book, *It's Not a Glass Ceiling it's a Sticky Floor.* The focus of her Women in Leadership and Learning (WILL) program is to help women address the beliefs, assumptions, and self-defeating behaviors that hold them back. [66]

> *"Competency development is not as important as truly understanding that self-awareness is one of the keys to advancement and that many women already possess the skills for the next level. It is more of a self-limiting bias that they have about themselves.*

Once a woman has freed herself from life's sticky floors there's nowhere to go but up."

The second challenge of a women's development curriculum within organizations is that it only focuses on enhancing a woman's skill set. Many of the clients I work with have stand-alone women's high potential development programs. Routinely they will bring women into the corporate office, give them a 360-degree feedback and personal coaching, and place them in some type of development assignment. At the end the program, they then send them back to the Field or some remote location. Sadly, the advancement rate of these high potential women is rarely in line with what the company's goals are, and it focuses on one critical area: a "fix the women" mindset.

What is missing is any development or accountability for the male leaders to whom these women ultimately report. The reality is that men and women view leadership competencies differently. Organizations can provide all the coaching, support, and nurturing of women possible, but if they do not address and hold accountable their leaders (often men) for advancing their women, they are wasting their time and money.

The key to successful high potential programs for women is to engage their male leaders at the same time and educate men to understand and appreciate different leadership styles and behaviors.

In this manner when women and their male leaders return to the workplace they have a shared understanding and accountability. The role and significance of engaging male champions will be the focus of Chapter 9.

The Succession Planning Paradox: A Peek behind the Curtain

In addition to the staffing challenges faced, organizations are often reluctant to discuss true succession planning. Many organizations struggle to even use the phrase "high potential" as they do not want to inflate an employee's perception that they may be on a short list to advancement. Succession planning, specifically targeting women, is absolutely critical and it needs to take place at the most senior level of the organizations.

If the senior leadership team is not looking three to four levels down into the organization and questioning why women are not being interviewed for manager and director positions, they're failing to fill the pipeline for the next generation of leaders. Formal succession planning at multiple levels is not solely an HR responsibility—it includes a commitment embraced by senior leadership.

Try this experiment in your organization. Create a presentation deck with the pictures of the top 50 to 100 leaders in all of your departments. Now, place pictures of the next two people in line to replace your leaders.

In my experience . . .

**You'll see about 80 percent of men looking
back at you. This is what your company will look
like in the next five years.**

The question is not whether this is right or wrong, but rather do these images truly reflect the markets that you serve, and the best and most available talent in the marketplace? While this seems so simple an exercise, the visual optics are truly eye-opening and will help senior leaders begin to understand and internalize what their pipeline looks like.

To summarize our chapter, there are dozens of HR programs and processes that need to be examined through a lens of gender. I've examined seven HR paradoxes that I believe are critical and are not being discussed in a robust manner in most organizations. I would encourage you to have this conversation and continue to add to this list as I know you will come up with your own organizational paradoxes.

Getting this right is not simply found by solving the HR Paradox and Organizational Paradox. It can only be truly successful when talent is owned by all leaders in the organization. I will continue to explore the final elements critical to advancing women with a critical eye on senior leadership's responsibility in our next chapter, The Leadership Imperative.

Summary Points from Chapter 6

- For companies to truly to "win with all employees," HR programs and processes need to be understood and embraced by all leaders and managers in the organization.

- Research is showing the need to have non-gender biased language in job descriptions.

- Companies need to examine their compensation practices and insure they are both fair and equitable as a significant portion of a woman's pay gap starts with her reluctance to negotiate a salary upon joining the company.

- When it comes to the subjective nature of performance management, we would like to think that all managers are gender-blind and color-blind. Unfortunately, this is not always the case. Men and women assessed talent differently and this impacts performance assessment, selection, and succession.

- Successful Gender Training programs present the business case and economic value of gender diversity as well as how to acknowledge and leverage gender dynamics.

- Effective Business Resource Groups must be viewed as value added opportunities to support the business. Conduct pulse surveys and focus groups with your BRGs. And as with any other element of the business, hold your BRGs accountable to delivering value to the business. More importantly, your BRGs can serve to deepen the cultural competency of that specific group within the broader workforce population.

- Leadership development programs focused on women must move from a "fix the women" mindset to a "fix the culture and mindset" and engage male leaders as well.

- Senior leadership must embrace true succession planning and examine what the organization looks like beyond just the next level of potential talent.

WHY WOMEN Readiness Assessment

1. Regarding Recruitment, are all of your HR programs and processes both fair and equitable? If you examine job descriptions, are the words gender neutral? Is your compensation strategy equitable to women?

2. Regarding Retention, what are the processes in place to eliminate subjectivity in your Performance Management system? Are you conducting ongoing diagnostics to insure equitable ratings by gender and race? What elements of Diversity Training are driving true culture change? Are you leveraging your Business Resource Groups to drive bottom line results?

3. Is your women's development strategy focused on an approach of "fix the women" versus an approach of holding both men and women accountable? Is your leadership engaged in true succession planning and looking at least two levels down in the organization?

Deepening Your Learning

— *Book* —

Women Don't Ask: The High Cost of Avoiding Negotiation—And Positive Strategies for Change, Linda Babcock and Sara Laschever

— *Online Article* —

"Evidence that Gendered Wording in Job Advertisements Exists and Sustains Gender Inequality," *Journal of Personality and Social Psychology* (2011)

— *Website* —

http://www.diversitybestpractices.com

Chapter 7

The Leadership Imperative

"Being responsible sometimes means pissing people off."

— Colin Powell, On Leadership [67]

> *It was a number of years ago and I was attending one of my first-ever national diversity conferences. "We're on a diversity journey. Our company set forth a strategy a number of years ago and now, ten years into our ongoing pursuit, we're starting to see progress made in the advancement and retention of women. We've grown the percentage of women by almost 40 percent and now women represent almost 30 percent of our leadership and 18 percent of our C-suite. We have a long way to go, but we're getting there!"*

I recall those words, enthusiastically voiced by a Chief Diversity Officer. At first I was encouraged. It was good to know that companies were making progress, setting strategies, and measuring success. Yet, as I listened on, I became more and more disheartened. It had taken that company 10 years to drive a 40 percent increase, yet women were only 30 percent of leadership. Researching this further, I would come to find that this pretty much represented today's best-in-class companies. Most companies today are well behind that number.

Something else dawned on me that day; it was that diversity officer's use of the word "journey." That word was echoed by many of the people in attendance that day—brilliant, hard-working diversity practitioners defining their effort in advancing more women and minorities as a journey.

I still hear that word used today to describe how companies are undertaking their gender diversity initiatives. And every time I do, I think back to my days in sales and how the field approached their goals and initiatives.

I have never been on a "sales journey."
If you don't make your sales goals for two quarters,
you're probably going to get fired!

People go on journeys, organizations implement long-term strategic plans. Diversity practitioners, human resource professionals, and organizations must change this dialogue to be much more powerful and to demonstrate action and accountability. Senior leaders need to stop saying journey, and instead say "we are on year two of our five-year strategic diversity plan and as a result we have accomplished . . . ."

Please don't get me wrong. I currently spend my life working in diversity and human resource management with some of the most wonderful and well-intended people on the planet. Yet progress is still moving at a snail's pace today. We must make a mindset change; we must move from using hopeful words like "journey" to more urgent words like "imperative."

As you'll recall from our YWomen Integrated Women's Leadership Framework, the role of senior leadership sits at the top right corner. As with all quadrant analyses, success always resides in the upper right quadrant. To be successful with women's advancement, visible and vocal senior leadership commitment is the single-most important driver in the entire framework. This chapter is for senior leadership teams that reside in that top right quadrant and it identifies the four critical elements that every senior leadership team needs to accomplish in that role:

1. Treat Women as a Business Imperative

2. Ask Tough Questions and Hold People Accountable

3. Demonstrate Commitment and Urgency

4. Deepen their Understanding of the Issues to Breaking the 16% barrier

Treat Women as a Business Imperative

In Chapter 2, I introduced three business reasons to create an Integrated Women's Leadership Strategy: to grow revenue, to improve operating profit, and to enhance company reputation.

As with all business imperatives, it's critical for organizations to craft a strategic integrated plan for women just as they would any other business imperative.

This written plan must follow the exact template, framework, or process that your organization uses for your annual business planning process.

This seems intuitive if you approach women as a true business initiative, yet most organizations do not take this approach. The reality is: it's absolutely critical that the organization understands that their women's leadership strategy needs to be treated as any other strategic imperative. This is the key to ownership by the entire organization as well as integration into the day-to-day work and processes of the organization.

One challenge that always surfaces is an organization's reluctance to assign hard quantitative and qualitative metrics into their Women's Leadership Scorecard. If your women's strategy is treated as a business imperative, then the initiatives will flow from your division's goals and strategies. And actionable tactics on the measures and metrics should then become self-apparent. The challenge for organizations that do not create truly integrated strategies is the execution of a series of unrelated activities and immeasurable tactics. Clearly linked strategies, initiatives, and metrics are critical to managing the successful implementation of your plan.

> ***"If you can't measure it, you can't manage it."***
> ***— Peter Drucker*** [68]

Measures and Metrics

DiversityInc has been studying companies' diversity metrics for more than a decade. They identify four stages of diversity management. [69]

1. **Stage One: Celebration-Focused -** The company has begun to recognize the value of diversity and begins to have celebrations, such as Women's History Month and the occasional guest speaker.

2. **Stage Two: Workforce-Focused -** The company has created a diversity plan—with actions, objectives, and milestones. It has begun to show gains in the diversity of its workforce and has implemented resource groups and, often, a structured mentoring program. The company now has a competitive advantage—with talent and reaching customers/clients—over competitors still in Stage One.

3. **Stage Three: Marketplace-Focused -** The organization has metrics-driven accountability for its diversity-management efforts, often through its executive diversity council. Its human capital and supplier diversity metrics are well above average and the company assesses and communicates clearly the value diversity management is bringing to the organization. These companies outpace their competitors in raising cultural competency in marketing and sales efforts.

4. **Stage Four: Out-Thinking Competition -** These companies leverage diversity management to create, sponsor, and nurture innovation. They provide thought-leadership and integrate cultural competency in all they do, from recruiting to customer service.

DiversityInc believes most companies are in the first two stages, with companies that earn high marks on the upper portions of The DiversityInc Top 50 Companies for Diversity list in Stage Three. It also notes that a handful of very innovative companies are poised to break into Stage Four.

A true Integrated Women's Leadership Strategy will incorporate Stages One through Three and by nature should move your company into Stage Four.

The following lists a few elements of a brief example of a Women's Leadership Scorecard. It includes strategies initiatives and metrics in the areas of revenue, engagement, and talent.

Integrated Women's Leadership Scorecard

Objective: Women's Business Initiative to generate incremental revenue growth of XX% resulting in an additional $XX MM in Operating Profit (Year One Annual Business Plan as a part of a Five Year Operating Business Plan)

Goal	Strategy	Initiative	Metric
From Sales and Marketing Plan			
• Grow market share of existing products by 10 points to the "Fast Tracker" target audience	• Implement breadth and depth targeted social media approach	• Execute "Women 365" (breadth marketing/social media plan) to target daily messaging as "a key part of your everyday life?" • Execute "Celebrate Now" (depth programming) targeted to twice a month indulgence	• 25% increase in sales of non-discounted full margin product • Increase of Favorite Brand rating by 6 points • 35% increase in sales of targeted discount dollars and products
• Acquire 1.2 MM new users via new product line targeted to "Fulfilled Empty Nester"	• Expand test market of "Project Ziva" nationally	• Sell-in of complete product line in Top 100 accounts • Execute targeted awareness trial program in top 20 markets by April	• $XX MM operating profit by year end • 15% targeted household penetration by June in top 20 markets
From Talent Plan			
• Double the number of women in senior leadership (Job Grades 4 and above) to 70 in 5 years. This year's goal is +10 new promotions	• Develop accelerated female leadership program	• Conduct analysis of promotions, losses, and chokepoints. Review data and implement solutions • Conduct talent review to determine high-potential talent. Source externally as needed to fill pipeline • Implement formal male engagement strategy	• Female talent movement numbers, promotions, regrettable losses • Internal vs. external Hires • 35 program attendees
• Increase engagement level of female employees by 12 points	• Implement formal flex time across Division	• Create flex-time policy, guidelines and implementation plan • Conduct management training on policy implementation	• Overall increase in engagement • Usage by role/function • 80% Completion rate
From Corporate Reputation Plan			
• Become our industry's top company for women	• Benchmark and exceed current industry competitors	• Obtain independent third-party analysis of our current state vs. competition • Conduct internal gap analysis for quick win and longer term elements	• Project milestones per plan • Change in external ranking

This does not represent a complete plan but merely a sampling of various elements

159

A complete Integrated Women's Leadership Scorecard necessarily includes elements from marketing, sales, supply chain, human resources and talent, procurement, engagement, company reputation, and corporate communications. An expanded listing of elements that companies are choosing to track and measure is included in the Appendix.

Every organization will be different. If you are not tracking elements now start small. If you are in Stage One, what can you add to move into Stage Two? If you are at Stage Two what additional Talent Metrics can you add and what Stage Three Marketplace elements can you add? Wherever you are organizationally you need to think incrementally and focus on integration. If you include this in your standard annual planning process it will ideally reflect the rest of your corporate initiatives. Finally, the best plans are not merely written and measured at headquarters but are pushed down to the most meaningful parts of the business.

One great example of integrating strategies, devising metrics, and pushing shared responsibility and accountability down through the organization is published in Walgreens Diversity & Inclusion Report, *Living Our Commitment: Diversity, Inclusion, and Engagement.* [70]

At Walgreens, division-specific action plans are designed to highlight specific, measurable, attainable, and relevant strategies in three key areas:

1. Culture – communications, training, and employee engagement

2. Accountability - scorecards, strategy, and affirmative action/compliance

3.   Partnership - talent acquisition, talent development, business resource groups and networks, disability inclusion, and supplier diversity

Writing a strategic plan is important; building a scorecard of measures and metrics is critical. Hard metrics that are quantitatively measured are obviously the best. Sales results, success of initiatives, and recruitment and advancement can all easily be tracked.

I will acknowledge that not all of the programs and processes regarding women will have hard, quantifiable measurements. The inability to measure and track initiatives can be a challenging activity, particularly regarding certain staff functions or strategies that do not have hard metrics. As with similar areas in your business, you may in fact have to take a qualitative approach. This must not keep organizations from establishing goals, strategies, and action plans. Then ultimately, it becomes the role of senior leadership to drive those initiatives and hold the organization accountable in whatever manner possible.

At almost every conference that I attend, invariably three key questions come up regarding measures and metrics. This is how I confidently and honestly answer each:

Can we really measure that? YES.
Will we get in trouble for measuring that? MAYBE.
Can we really hold people accountable? YES.

Ask Tough Questions and Hold People Accountable

I started this chapter with the Colin Powell quote, "Being responsible sometimes means pissing people off." The operative phrase here is "being responsible." Those who are responsible or accountable in an organization have a broader view of things, and the higher up the organization, the broader that view becomes.

Peers and subordinates who don't share your perspective on the business and your scope of accountability will often not understand the reasons and implications for why certain strategies and initiatives are undertaken. And some are going to get "pissed off," as General Powell puts it, when they can't make that connection.

The following section of this book regarding measures, metrics, and holding people accountable will be the single-most contentious part when implementing your plan and as such the most important for everyone to understand.

Asking tough questions and holding people accountable are two primary roles of leaders. At the end of the day, the accountability for the success of any initiative in your organization rests with its leaders. Yet when it comes to talking about women, most organizations are scared to death to put measures and metrics in place.

"I can't set hard metrics on promoting women. That will open us up for potential litigation and there will be no end to the 'white male backlash' I'll experience."

These issues of (1) hard metrics and the potential for litigation, (2) the perceived organizational backlash, and (3) accountability for the initiatives, are some of the biggest challenges holding back many organizations. Much of it stems from confusing the word metric as a "quota" which, in the absence of understanding value, creates a whole host of issues.

If your company is still talking about quotas, it's time for you to move into this new century. Quotas were originally established for vendors that had the government as their client. Government vendors were required (and still are) to submit periodic reports indicating the required a minimum number of women or minorities on their staffs to win an RFP from a government agency or to keep that account active. Unfortunately, this word "quota" has weaved its way into the general business language. The problem it, it's come to represent a goal without speaking to its purpose.

Quotas are about having a *minimum* number of a certain group of people in your workforce. Accountable metrics is about *maximizing* your organization's efforts to mirror the available marketplace opportunity and available talent.

This mind shift from minimizing to maximizing is absolutely critical for organizations to be successful. Progressive companies are reframing their conversation and moving from words like "quotas" to "goals or aspirations," and in doing so, redefining the intent of their organizations—not to just have women in their ranks, but to win with all their employees, and an increasingly diverse marketplace.

There are still many sides to the conversation and even the usage varies from company to company. In a recent study conducted for the Society for Human Resource Management (SHRM) by the Economist

Intelligence Unit, one quote by a chief inclusion and diversity officer said,

> "By 2020, we want to have 25 percent of executive positions filled by women. We are also setting 'aspirational guidelines' for people with an international background for our management team. I don't worry about using 'the Q word.' So many people are against quotas, but if you have a better idea how to measure progress toward achieving Diversity, feel free to share it with me." [71]

My goal is for your organization not to get caught up in the semantics of the word "quota." Measures, metrics, and aspirational goals are easily substituted and allow for a reframing of the conversation. The desired outcome is to have a meaningful business dialogue.

Without metrics and accountability you cannot successfully build an organization with the best talent that mirrors its marketplace.

Metrics and the Potential for Litigation

Many companies today have goals for the recruitment, retention, and advancement of women. They do use words like "targets," "goals," and "guidelines." The issue that most companies encounter when wanting to directly track their goals is a reluctance often expressed by their legal counsel, "If we track it, it will become discoverable in a lawsuit." In their defense, they are charged with keeping the company safe from litigation. Here is what I've discovered though that is at the crux of most of the lawsuits in this area:

***The issue is not whether you track or not;
the issue is that once you discover there is an issue, are you
in fact taking action on the problem?***

Most litigation today comes from a failure to do the hard work to ensure fairness and equity. If you track diversity metrics and in fact find out that there are systemic diversity issues embedded in your programs and processes and you fail to do anything about it, then you will face litigation. My belief is that,

Many organizations fail to track and monitor because they in fact know that they have a problem and choose to do nothing about it.

Ignoring the problem is not a successful winning strategy. This key point separates companies that have turned the corner and are winning with women from those that have not. As you will discover later in this chapter, best-in-class companies are choosing to not only track and hold people accountable, but they are also tying significant compensation to the achievement of those goals.

Does tracking and holding people accountable help minimize organizational backlash? The surprising answer is yes, if it's done correctly. By tracking, measuring, and holding people accountable while at the same time demonstrating transparency in your programs and processes, you can actually minimize the potential for backlash.

Does this mean that backlash does not exist at best-in-class companies? No, of course it exists, and there will always be pockets of individuals in the organization that do not fully support their companies' strategies. A closer look at the complete transparency of numbers if often the best solution.

Transparency and Organizational Backlash

The concern that the tracking of the advancement of women (or minorities) will result in men being left behind is just not true at an organizational level. While pockets may exist and mistakes may occur, the truth is that most organizational numbers do not back up this claim.

> *Even in most companies that have aggressive plans in place to advance women, almost two-thirds of promotions still go to men.*

If you don't believe this, check with your organization's HR department. Referencing again the SHRM study, another chief diversity officer said,

> *"Concerning reverse discrimination, there is always that element and we have to be careful. But the fact remains that most opportunities are filled by members of the majority group. Representation of women and minorities in higher positions is a fraction of their proportion of the population in general.* [72]

This lack of transparency, an unwillingness to share the actual numbers, and an apprehension to take action is also lost in the persistent zero-sum-game dialogue around quotas that we discussed earlier. Organizations not having a solid understanding of the business case and rationale behind why they should endeavor to promote women oftentimes compound the issue in their hiring processes.

Managers, inadequately trained in the rationale for hiring a female, are often ill-prepared to provide the necessary feedback to a male who doesn't get the job.

Too often, when a woman receives a promotion over a man, the failure within the organization is often caused by the hiring manager's unwillingness to have an honest conversation with the man being passed over on why he didn't get hired. It's not uncommon for a male hiring manager to take the easy way out and tell the disadvantaged fellow,

> *"The only reason she was promoted over you is because the company wants to advance more women."*

The truth is, companies that have complete transparency in their hiring, retention, and advancement programs recognize that men are still landing a clear majority of the promotions. It is only in developing accountability throughout the process that the entire system will work.

Tying Accountability to Compensation

In successful companies, leadership makes a fundamental shift in philosophy for the organization and says, "This is important, it's a business imperative, and we are going to track it." If we examine the companies that participated in the annual DiversityInc survey, tying the performance of your diversity initiatives to compensation is a common best practice of the top fifty. [73]

Here are examples of what some of those companies are doing:

- At Novartis, the number one company in the Diversity Top 50, the executive leadership team's annual performance management goals include a 20 percent weighting toward people-related objectives, which include specific diversity objectives.

- Number two, Sodexo, (also a Catalyst award winner) ties 25 percent of top executives' and up to 15 percent of senior managements' bonus compensation directly to diversity goals— and these are paid regardless of the financial performance of the company.

- Kaiser Permanente, number four out of fifty, links 15 percent of senior-executive compensation to diversity metrics.

In fact, of those reporting their diversity metrics to DiversityInc,

> **W** Seventy-six percent of the DiversityInc Top 50 specifically state that they tie some form of compensation or performance management to the achievement of their diversity metrics. [74] That number represents the companies that specifically spoke to the issue of compensation. The actual percentage is probably higher.

Demonstrate Commitment and Urgency

If, as leaders, we've written the business plan, are asking the tough questions, and are holding people accountable, then the last missing element is implementing that plan by demonstrating commitment to the organization with an absolute sense of urgency.

Imagine for a moment that you've just completed writing your organization's annual business plan and you are presenting it to your Board of Directors or the investment community.

You begin your presentation with a story about the journey your company is on, followed by weak strategies and soft metrics. In summarizing your talk, you close with, " . . . and we will be implementing this, oh, I don't know, sometime in the next eighteen months." It's likely you would not keep your job or the confidence of your shareowners for very long. A senior leader's key role is to focus the organization, garner the resources, and implement the plan with a sense of commitment and urgency.

Without your absolute commitment, visible advocacy, and a sense of urgency, you will continue to talk about advancing women for years and never take meaningful action.

The Role of the CEO and Senior Leadership Team

If you were to look at the single number one contributor on virtually every list of best practices for organizations that are winning with women, it would be the visible and verbal commitment of the CEO and senior leadership team. Both must have a mindset that, above all else, understands the value in having and pursuing diversity initiatives. It then becomes the responsibility of senior leadership to express that mindset in their actions to effect true change.

The Role of the CEO

The role of the CEO is to demonstrate clear vision, present and defend the business case, and express his or her plans for growth through change. CEOs act with a sense of urgency and resolve.

It is the singular commitment of senior leadership that forces a change in mindset from compliance to commitment.

What does visible commitment look like? According to Diversity Best Practices, the top five ways that CEOs show commitment to diversity are as follows: [75]

> **W** Eighty-one percent of companies have CEOs who require their diversity executives to report workforce diversity metrics directly to them.
>
> **W** Seventy-seven percent have CEOs who support having a CEO workforce diversity statement on the company website and in other corporate materials.
>
> **W** Seventy-seven percent have CEOs who meet regularly with the organization's workforce diversity executives.
>
> **W** Sixty-nine percent of companies provide annual updates on workplace diversity to their company's boards of directors.
>
> **W** Fifty-four percent have CEOs who include workplace diversity-related information in annual updates with employees.

And while the CEO's voice of commitment is absolutely critical, we cannot overstate the importance of the entire senior leadership team being able to recite the same story.

The Role of the Leadership Team

The role of the leadership team is to be completely aligned with the CEO on this subject and exhibit the same sense of urgency and resolve in their actions and behaviors. They must be willing to walk the talk and create cultural change. This is the only way to ensure credibility in their divisions and departments and with their teams. They must develop the plans, establish milestones, and proactively present progress to the CEO and company.

The questions to ask of your senior leadership team include:

Are they capable of articulating the business case on a daily basis?

Are they integrating dialogue points into operating plans, divisional communications, and even staff meetings?

Are they putting solid metrics in place to drive accountability?

The role of every senior leader cannot be underestimated for it is critical at that level to drive the strategy programs and processes down into middle management and through to the remainder of the organization. Obtaining middle manager buy-in and its significance will be explored further in Chapter 9.

Breaking the 16 Percent Barrier - The Top One Percent is Not about Performance

A final consideration for senior leadership is to truly understand the issues, challenges, and barriers that women face in making it to the C-suite. In Chapters 5 and 6, a number of Field issues and HR programs and processes were discussed. These are baseline programs that are critical to advancing all talented people. However, as we examine women as a leadership imperative, we must add one discussion point to truly getting more women into the C-suite. The last critical element is for senior leaders to truly understand, and take ownership for breaking this barrier.

As we first examined in The Field Factor, line leaders must truly understand and appreciate all of the issues, opportunities, and landmines that women face. This mindset is critical to solving the pipeline issue for women that leads to senior leadership. There's no question that even if you are the best of the best, sometimes it takes a significant amount of exposure, sponsorship, and yes, even a little luck, to get to the top.

Revisiting the Careers of Victor and Evelyn

Ten years have now lapsed since Victor and Evelyn, along with eight other colleagues, joined the company. Their cohort group of six men and four women has been thinned by 60 percent, leaving three men and no women, aside from Evelyn. The organization has gone through a series of restructures, stripping out layers of middle managers. Victor and Evelyn both endured a series of lateral moves and had to bear two more rounds of relocation as a result of

> *reorganizations. Yet, both continued to produce great results. Victor has moved into a Regional Vice President's job and has reunited with Scott who is now Divisional President. Evelyn has been promoted to Director.*

Performance is a Given

As I said before, the Field is tough and filled with multiple relocations, challenging customers, constant reorganizations, and unrelenting business demands. In our story above, you can see that, barring any unforeseen circumstances, it appears Victor is on his way to the C-suite and quite frankly, odds are that Evelyn isn't.

Well, believe it or not, the odds are, neither is Victor. You see . . .

In a company of 150,000 employees, if you're performance is in the top one percent, there are 1,500 people just as talented as you are.

Depending on the company, there are ten to twenty actual C-level positions. Even if we expand senior leader roles to the top one percent of positions in our organization, that suggests there are approximately 148,500 people competing for 1,500 jobs in senior management.

Getting into that top one percent is really, really tough!

It's about Performance and Connections

Every successful woman (and man for that matter) wants to be known for being promoted as a result of her hard work and perseverance.

However, hard work and resolve are just two of the criteria necessary to move ahead.

Returning to our research from *The Sponsor Effect*, by Sylvia Ann Hewlett et al. shows the differences in where women and men place emphasis on what it takes to get ahead:

Women . . .

> **W** Seventy-seven percent believe that what drives promotion at their firm is a combination of hard work, long hours, and education credentials.
>
> **W** Of those who have advanced, 72 percent credit their track record for their most recent promotion, as opposed to 48 percent who credit personal connections.

Men . . .

> **W** Eighty-three percent readily acknowledge that "who you know" counts for a lot, or at least as much as "how well you do your job."
>
> **W** Fifty-seven percent credit their recent advancement to personal connections. [76]

Many women tend to feel that getting ahead based on "connections" is a dirty tactic and that hard work alone is their ticket to the top while men knowingly work within those given often unwritten rules and feel much more comfortable working their connections.

Mentors, Advocates, and Sponsors

Let's peer once more into the career development of Victor and Evelyn. As you'll recall from Chapter 5,

> *As a result of Victor's relationship with his boss Scott and great coaching from Mark, Victor was exposed to multiple opportunities for special projects.*
>
> *Evelyn's boss, Ron, didn't see significant leadership potential in her, and when opportunities for special projects arose, he didn't consider nominating her. Evelyn assumed that by keeping her head down and working even harder, she would eventually be noticed.*
>
> *Victor and Evelyn's company did not have a formal mentoring program. Still Victor found a way to build a relationship with Mark who provided valuable coaching. Additionally, Victor was eager to take advantage of social opportunities whereas Evelyn still regarded them as frivolous.*

It's been well-documented and proven time and again that a formal mentoring program is critical for the development of your talent. Typically, mentors are of a higher rank and work in a similar operational area as you do. What is evolving today is the need for people to have multiple mentors, each providing functional expertise. Moreover, if you are truly wanting to build your business mindset you should attempt to have mentors in a host of areas such as finance, marketing, supply chain, and any other area that is important to help build a strategic mindset around the organization. While mentoring is important, it is just the beginning and, in itself, is simply not enough.

A greater value to a person's advancement that's not often discussed is the role of an Advocate and a Sponsor. An Advocate is someone who typically knows the associate well. He (I say "he" because the clear majority of advocates and sponsors are male) may have played a mentoring role in the past but is now willing to speak up for and promote an associate for special projects, assignments, and other high profile leadership development activities.

Advocates are typically known by the associate and in many circumstances a personal friendship may actually exist. Advocates are also people in key roles who are willing to promote you and your talents. Typically, they have been a past manager that you worked for early in your career and they were very impressed with your abilities. Advocates also serve to increase your exposure in the company and will often make introductions to other key people in the organization. This "informal endorsement" is a key outcome from increased exposure by your advocate.

Sponsors are very similar to advocates but in fact sit at "The Talent Table." These are people who are willing to bet their career on your success. They pull up their chair and make declarative statements such as, "I believe Victor is the right fit for this job." They see something in you and they want pull you up and challenge you with new opportunities. They believe your style and leadership will help sustain the organization's success.

Unfortunately, many women underestimate the role that sponsorship plays in their career. As a result, many high-performing women who could make perfect leaders simply don't have the sponsorship needed to advance.

An additional challenge is that male senior leaders are often apprehensive about sponsoring a woman candidate. The reasons vary from not recognizing the value in her performance and style of leadership, to feeling more comfortable sponsoring another man whose skills and abilities "remind me of me when I was younger."

Much of the missed opportunity is in women's reluctance to seek out sponsors and advocates, partly because of their driving need to prove themselves, and partly for another interesting reason.

In 2009, The Hidden Brain Drain task force launched a study commissioned by American Express, Deloitte, Intel, and Morgan Stanley to determine the impact of sponsorship and why women fail to make better use of it. The study not only found that women underestimate the value of sponsorship to their advancement, but those who do understand its importance fail to cultivate it. [77]

This mindset, which was discussed in Chapter 5 regarding middle managers continued to play itself out in women of high responsibility. Do you have a relationship with someone above you that is so strong that they will go to bat for you as an advocate for your promotion? As a rising woman are you cultivating an advocate or a sponsor? Is your view of using connections holding you back?

These are all questions to ponder. And as if that isn't enough to hold women back there is one more element that is rarely researched in reaching the C-suite.

And a Little Luck

We have looked at the importance of performance and exposure, the value of meritocracies and sponsorship, and the blind spots that both men and women have in those last two necessary conditions for advancement. Yet, there is often one factor that is not talked about: luck!

Luck is defined by many as preparedness meeting opportunity.

Are the people who ascend to the very highest rungs of the organization just a little bit luckier in their ascent than their equally brilliant peers? It is an interesting question to ponder. Most men and women in the C-suite distinguish themselves very early on and often in their careers. This puts them on a trajectory to gain incremental assignments and larger opportunities than afforded their peers. They also skillfully surrounded themselves with people who supported them and they in turn returned that favor in trust and support.

During this ascent, there is a high likelihood that they encountered other successful people, perspective advocates, and sponsors who could potentially pull them up later. Additionally, most senior leaders very early in their career also happened to work for another rising star. We see this all the time in organizations; corporate insiders call it a regime strategy. Each time a new senior leader takes over, he or she gets the opportunity to bring in his or her own team.

This notion of being on the right team is absolutely critical to the advancement of women. This is when preparedness in fact meets opportunity. It is only through leaders and their organizations truly understanding the key interdependencies of performance, exposure, succession planning, special developmental opportunities, fair and equitable pay, performance management systems, and a host of other factors that will keep women in the pipeline and have them available to be in the right place at the right time.

If we reflect back on the women who are currently sitting in CEO roles, all were equally prepared when opportunities presented themselves. This is not to say that any of the women sitting in the C-suites of corporate America were merely lucky; all clearly earned their position in the organization. All were well credentialed and had broad organizational and operating experience. And they learned how to create luck for themselves while in the Field.

The challenge and the opportunity for organizations, particularly given everything we've talked about regarding talent today, is to get really good at the preparedness part of the luck equation.

Summary Points from Chapter 7

- Everyone knows diversity is critically important to the success of the organization. Yet progress is still slow. We need a mindset change. People go on journeys, but organizations need to use more urgent words like "imperative."

- In order to *win with women*, every senior leadership team needs to embrace four critical actions:

  1. Treat Women as a Business Imperative

  2. Ask Tough Questions and Hold People Accountable

  3. Demonstrate Commitment and Urgency

  4. Deepen their Understanding of the Issues to Breaking the 16 Percent Barrier

- Companies must write integrated strategic leadership plans for women just as they do for every other functional area of the company. These plans must be tied to the business and have measurable outcomes.

- These issues of (1) hard metrics and the potential for litigation, (2) the perceived organizational backlash, and (3) accountability for the initiatives, may be the biggest challenges holding back many organizations. Much of it stems from the word "quota" which, in the absence of understanding value, creates a whole host of issues.

- Quotas are about having a minimum number of a certain group of people in your workforce. Success with women is about maximizing your organization's efforts to mirror the available marketplace opportunity and available talent.

- Data does not support the perception that men are being passed over for women. In most organizations, two-thirds of promotions still go to men.

- Best in class companies are tying executive compensation to hard diversity metrics.

- The role of the CEO and the senior leadership team to express their commitment and urgency through their own actions and commitments.

- Senior leadership must understand the additional barriers that women face in breaking into the highest ranks of the organization and the importance of advocates and sponsors.

WHY WOMEN Readiness Assessment

1. Does your organization have a sense of urgency regarding its women's leadership strategy and how is it being demonstrated? What elements are contained on your scorecard and at what level of the organization is the scorecard held accountable? How is it being pushed down to the middle management/operating units of your company?

2. Does your organization have hard metrics that it tracks regarding the recruitment, advancement, and retention of women and minorities? Do you publish the numbers to insure organizational transparency? Do the majority of your promotions still go to the largest majority employee population and is this being communicated to minimize backlash? Is compensation tied to a women's/diversity scorecard?

3. Do you and your leadership team understand the significant role that advocates and sponsors play in moving women into the most senior levels of the organization? What is your leadership doing to insure connections and exposure is being given to high potential women?

Deepening Your Learning

— *Book* —

The Inclusion Paradox: The Obama Era and the Transformation of Global Diversity, Andreas T. Tapia (2013)

— *Online Article* —

"Global Diversity and Inclusion: Perceptions, Practices, and Attitudes" SHRM (Society for Human Resource Management)

— *Website* —

http://www.diversityinc.com

Chapter 8

The Company Reputation Connection

"Executives operate under the mistaken belief that the public trusts them.

But CEOs are among the least trusted professions, just barely ahead of used-car dealers and politicians."

—Daniel Diermeier, Ph.D.,
Kellogg School of Business, *Reputation Rules* [78]

> *It was a few days before Christmas when I heard this "breaking news" headline,*
>
> *"A breach of credit and debit card data at discount retailer Target may have affected as many as 40 million shoppers who went to their stores during the three weeks following Thanksgiving."*

Working in women's leadership strategy, as I listened to the news I realized that this was even a bigger deal than just the loss of secured data. I stated earlier in the book that I believe Target has an amazing culture and truly understands women. But you see, this was not only a security breach, but a betrayal of trust. And to women who make their retailers a "preferred brand," trust is absolutely critical.

Over the next six months, it would become known that the credit and personal information of over 40 million credit and debit cardholders and the personal information of a staggering 70 million people had potentially been compromised. In an attempt to preserve its trust with their shoppers, Gregg Steinhafel, Target chairman, president, and CEO, made a statement,

"I know that it is frustrating for our guests to learn that this information was taken and we are truly sorry they are having to endure this." [79]

By May 2014, Gregg Steinhafel, a Target employee of thirty-five years, and his CIO, Beth Jacob, would end up resigning.

I'm certain that the night before this violation was discovered, Mr. Steinhafel was fully consumed with driving Christmas traffic through his stores. Little did he know that a security breach was in the offing that would end his long career with Target, which started when he was in the field as a merchandising trainee in 1979. Since this event at Target we've heard of numerous other breaches ranging from Home Depot to the now infamous Sony hack.

As if business today wasn't tough enough, your company reputation is also under constant siege. I opened the book by commenting on the three things that keep senior leaders up at night: growing revenue, improving operating profits, and enhancing your company reputation.

Of the three, the one that is the most likely to be openly assaulted (and the one you may have the least amount of control over) in today's world is your company reputation.

What does this have to do with women? Well,

Since women control 85 percent of the spending in this country, it's fair to say that at least 85 percent of your company's reputation is in their hands as well.

Buying products and services is more than transactional with women. Their preference is to develop brand relationships, and companies that are attuned to this reciprocate by building and maintaining relationships with their female customers in every way possible—most importantly in how they communicate with women.

When formulating the YWomen Integrated Women's Leadership Framework, the "why" and "how" of Company Reputation needs to be examined with utmost attention given to the last key element for success—an Integrated Communications Plan for both internal and external stakeholders. For this reason, the "connection" I make in this chapter is essentially between Company Reputation and Integrated Communications, specifically 1) the elements of trust, 2) corporate social responsibility, and 3) an importance to all stakeholders, especially women, to have an integrated communications plan. These three components form the tenets of The Company Reputation Connection.

The Elements of Trust

To understand a company's reputation, especially through the eyes of women constituents, we need to revisit this concept of trust. We've talked about multiple factors that impact trust in the marketplace and the fact that most consumers are just not as trusting as they used to be. To win with women, companies would stand to benefit by taking a much deeper look at the drivers of trust.

Dr. Daniel Diermeier at the Kellogg School of Business outlines four key dimensions of trust: [80]

- Transparency
- Expertise
- Commitment
- Empathy

Diermeier is an expert in crisis management and his curriculum centers on how companies can best go about managing their affairs in times of absolute crisis. I believe his model serves as a great checklist to better define your strategy for building trust with women.

Building a Model of Trust

Target's unfortunate records breach that I opened the chapter with is a great example of a company under crisis.

- How did they respond?
- Did they say the right things to demonstrate urgency, transparency, and expertise in dealing with the situation?

- Did they exhibit a sense of commitment, and most importantly for women, did they genuinely express empathy?

In his book, *Reputation Rules: Strategies for Building Your Company's Most Valuable Asset*, Diermeier explains it this way:

> *"Corporate reputation strategies have direct and measurable effects on the evaluation of core brand attributes. They can affect overall customer perceptions, evaluations of corporate logos, and even opinions of product taste and levels of consumption. Corporate executives are largely unaware of such effects."* [81]

Diermeier utilizes a "Trust Radar" as a visual demonstration of the four critical areas organizations must center on and address when crises arise. [82]

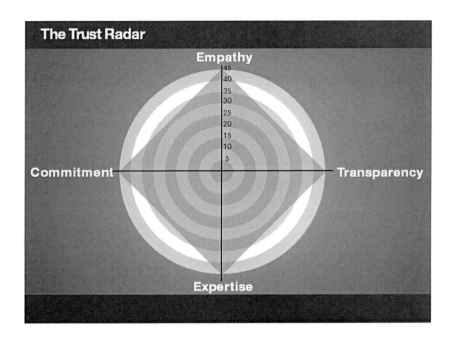

In order to safeguard against any emergency that may surface, a company must actively make efforts to manage its image with all its constituents. In other words, any enterprise hoping to sustain its persona in the marketplace must engage in "reputation management."

Transparency, Expertise, Commitment, and Empathy

In the summer of 2014, literally within weeks of each other, Google, Yahoo, Facebook, and Twitter each released their diversity report card documenting the makeup and profile of their employee populations. Not surprisingly, the results mirrored most other tech companies with well over 80 percent of employees being white and Asian males. My bringing this up is not to challenge these four companies on their numbers and profile, but more importantly to understand why. Why did they release these reports? Why then?

Like many companies, they could keep their diversity reports to themselves, put programs in place, and try their best to improve things. The answer is simple: transparency and company reputation. Tech companies are being taken to task for resembling little more than grown-up fraternity houses. I believe they chose to release their numbers now because they're in the early stages of a talent crisis.

By taking this action, they're voluntarily forcing themselves to improve. They're taking their business case public and this will allow them to immediately begin holding people accountable for driving change. As I discussed earlier,

Transparency in your numbers is the first critical test of demonstrating your commitment to women.

The areas of Expertise and Commitment speak to a proficiency in being able to deal with the crisis and the pledge to solve it, not as an endless journey, but as an immediate imperative.

Creating global women's consuls and BRGs, bringing in outside speakers, participating in benchmarking with best-in-class companies, and then publishing diversity reports are significant demonstrations. Each shows that your organization gets it (*expertise*) and is executing programs to improve the existing situation (*commitment*). Growth companies don't just let their current or past reputation speak for itself. They constantly strive to improve how they're being perceived in the marketplace, and not allow their persona to stagnate, tarnish, or slide. They're being quite vocal about their intent and doing something about it in targeted ways through social media.

A good example of this is found in the oil and gas industry—a sector you wouldn't expect to find companies expressing their commitment to building their reputations with women. The competition is unbelievably high for top-of-class young women with degrees in chemical engineering and experienced women already in the field who are looking for more welcoming cultures in this previously all-male industry.

Companies such as Marathon Oil and BP have created targeted social media campaigns including YouTube videos of women as individual contributors, managers, and senior leaders. [83]

In these vignettes, women in various departments explain their role, their contribution to creating cleaner energy, and their happiness with their careers and the people on their teams. As you listen to these video vignettes, see how many times each of these women refers to their companies' reputations and how it aligns with their own identities and personal beliefs.

There are No Secrets!

The final reason to become committed to transparency is that there really are no secrets any longer in organizations. Given the advent of websites like Glassdoor.com, employees, advocate groups, or perspective employees can instantly glean information regarding your company. Are you a great place to work? Do you live your values? What is your compensation strategy? There literally are no secrets any longer and through the convergence of all types of social media, everyone knows the internal workings of your organization. Within a short amount of time, websites will begin to pop up that will allow employees to "rate my manager" or "rate my senior leadership team." These websites already exist in academia where students access websites and openly discuss and rate their professors. [84]

It's only a matter of time before your organization's company reputation is going to come under similar scrutiny. How would your leadership team pass an online assessment as to their ability?

Empathy is Not Sympathy

I hesitate to include the word *empathy* as a "test" for organizations as they build their company reputation with women because people tend to confuse empathy with sympathy. Empathy is the ability to mutually experience the thoughts, emotions, and direct experience of others and should not be confused with sympathy, which is a feeling of care and understanding for the suffering of others. Both words have similar usage but differ in their emotional meaning.

> *Women clearly do not want your sympathy, which can unintentionally show up as being condescending. They do increasingly want companies who understand the importance of empathy as a critical operating norm.*

Empathy, the ability and desire to understand situations and dynamics in a corporate setting, is a very appropriate test for your company reputation. True empathy is demonstrated as having a cultural competency around organizational issues that may otherwise stall the execution of your Integrated Women's Leadership Strategy. I will delve into this a bit more in our next chapter when we talk about creating male champions.

I started this section on trust by examining the Target security breach.

- How did they respond?
- Did they say the right things to demonstrate urgency, transparency, and expertise in dealing with the situation?
- Did they exhibit a sense of commitment, and most importantly for women—did they genuinely express empathy?

I believe the answer to all of these questions is yes . . . and the CEO still lost his job.

Organizations can no longer take a wait-and-see approach and hope that nothing goes awry. Many companies are being proactive every day. The opportunity is to insure it is being solidly linked to your Integrate Women's Leadership Strategy. Let's examine three specific types of activities that fall under the umbrella of Corporate Social Responsibility—community/philanthropy, corporate social programming, and supplier diversity—that also significantly impact women.

Corporate Social Responsibility

If you are a major organization today, you are engaged in a host of activities that also fall under the umbrella of company reputation. Each year, organizations support huge initiatives such as contributing to the United Way or the Susan G. Komen Race for the Cure for breast cancer, or any number of literally hundreds of types of activities. Why do companies do this?

Because it makes them better community and global citizens, and they know that there's a return for showing corporate responsibility.

This concept—the Triple-Bottom Line—of focusing not solely on its finances, but giving consideration to the company's social, economic, and environmental impact is accelerating in relevancy with companies. [85]

Though this concept has actually been around since the mid-1990s, the opportunity for women is insuring that your Women's Integrated Leadership Strategy is a connected and a visible part of your Corporate Social Responsibility (CSR) plan. Up until now, everything we talked about in the book has focused on driving business and improving your operating profit. Many companies still struggle with the notion of CSR activities. When we talk about areas such as community and philanthropy, we have to ask ourselves, is there a return on that investment and what is it? Many times, it's hard to quantify, yet organizations find reasons and ways to justify the expense—primarily because they feel it's the right thing to do. In a similar vein, it's an important thing to do for women.

Community/Philanthropy

Many of the best-in-class companies that we've already profiled are implementing aggressive philanthropy and community programs targeted at women.

- Walmart has launched its global initiative to source more products from local vendors with a primary focus on women-owned businesses.

- Coca-Cola has launched the program called "5 x 20" to help five million women by the year 2020 become entrepreneurs in developing countries.

- Target and a host of other retailers give a percentage of sales back to local communities that they serve.

- Walgreens offers many free local community health events.

Each of these initiatives serves as a great example of community-level involvement. It provides great connection points for their customers. As more women become suppliers and vendors to Walmart, they will naturally become loyal shoppers. As Coca-Cola creates miniature distributors with women-owned businesses, the community will grow and so will product sales in those communities across the globe.

Chances are, your company is already supporting women and communities through its philanthropic efforts. But have you ensured that all communications of those efforts connect back to your broader Integrated Women's Leadership Strategy?

Corporate Social Programming

I will use the term Corporate Social Programming to encompass all of the company programs around corporate conscience, corporate citizenship, sustainability, and the environment.

Let's take just one example. There are sensible monetary reasons for "going green." Even if you think global warming or climate changes are not real issues, all leaders agree that the cost of energy and water use are huge expenses for companies, especially in industries that rely heavily on those resources. Reducing those costs in this tight economy makes sense on two fronts: internally, it improves operating profit, while externally it bolsters the company's reputation as being environmentally aware and active.

Over the last ten years, corporations such as General Electric and Dow Chemical made drastic changes to their energy and recycling policies. What were initially responses to public pressure became permanent policies when they discovered the huge value in going green.

Since 3M instituted water and energy efficiencies across its enterprise, they have saved over $1 BILLION in operating expenses. [86]

Organizations that seek to attract and retain women should take notice. Corporate Social Programming is very important to women. Your future talent—many of whom are women—are looking for careers where they can be agents of positive change. This was the main finding of Net Impact's Talent Report: *What Workers Want.* [87]

Explains Liz Maw, the CEO of Net Impact,

> *"The 'What Workers Want' study clearly shows that women care deeply about having a job that makes an impact on social and environmental causes. We believe that if more employers focus on creating meaningful opportunities for employees to make a difference in the workplace — especially when it comes to traditional corporate jobs — we'll see more women with leadership roles in corporate America, a change that is sorely needed."*

Supplier Diversity

A final key element that connects and supports your company's reputation is your commitment to supplier diversity—a misunderstood concept that many firms have not truly embraced. Sometimes manufacturers implement diversity programs with their suppliers to meet customer mandates or federal supplier requirements, but I'm going beyond that.

Do you have a business case for establishing programs that support minority- and women-owned suppliers? Many large manufacturers say, "Yes." They've created supplier diversity programs that go beyond compliance. They've recognized that their supplier programs can help manufacturers connect with key segments in their customer base.

Manufacturers that have implemented supplier diversity programs say the payoff has come in the form of stronger relationships with their supply base, new business opportunities, and a more agile supply chain.

If we connect supplier diversity programs back to the women-owned business opportunities laid out in Chapter 3, we see tremendous economic potential to support both future customers and their communities.

To summarize, the Company Reputation Connection is just as important to your Women's Leadership Strategy as are marketplace and workplace results, sales and marketing operations, and human resources goals. Doing so must demonstrate a sense of transparency, expertise, commitment, and empathy. Our final opportunity is to help all internal and external stakeholders on connecting the dots on everything that your company is doing around women.

Integrated Communications Plan

Women are truly connected and many have vast relational networks. This is certainly not news. From an organizational standpoint, what's important to understand is not just the connectivity in their networks, but its connection to your brand and your reputation.

This connectivity is higher today than at any time in history. Just look at how quickly social media usage has grown. In 2008, 29 percent of online adults used social networking sites. Today—less than a decade later—that figure has more than doubled and is now 72 percent. [88]

W   Among Internet users, women are more likely to use Facebook, Pinterest, and Instagram than men are by ten percentage points. That equates to millions of consumers.

W   A roughly equal proportion of men and women use Twitter and Tumblr, though men are slightly heavier users of LinkedIn.

W   Today, 74 percent of women, when online, use social networking sites.

A parallel survey conducted by Women's Marketing Inc., and SheSpeaks sheds even more light on social media marketing and women. [89]

W   Forty percent of online women feel that the primary benefit of social media is to connect with family and friends.

W   Thirty-seven percent consider the primary benefit is being alerted to coupons, promotions, and deals by connecting with retailers and their products through their social media channels.

What's interesting are the general differences in the way and which males and females use social media. Facebook, Pinterest, and Instagram are about connecting with others. Twitter and Tumblr, preferred by men, are more about receiving content. [90]

The difference in male-female usage of LinkedIn—the business networking site—supports my earlier observation that men network for strategic reasons more often than women do.

Connecting and staying connected are at the very core of most women's online and offline strategies today. In her book, *Hustle: Marketing to Women in the Post-Recession World,* Bonnie Ullman talks about the personal relationship most women have with the things that bring them connectivity. [91]

In interviews with over 1,000 women, Bonnie learned that,

"*Women speak about their mobile devices, televisions, and computers as trusted companions . . . a woman's appetite for connectivity is nearly insatiable.*"

What are women talking about when on these sites? They're talking about their lives. They're talking about relationships. They're talking about things that are going well and sharing their challenges. And chances are they are talking about your company and your brands.

The desire to connect and stay connected shows itself even more so in a larger, global survey, by Barbara Annis & Associates of over 100,000 men and women leaders and managers on gender issues in the workplace and in their personal lives. [92]

> **W** Women on average, will tell thirty-two people of a good or bad experience, including strangers.
>
> **W** Men, on the other hand, will tell on average only up to three people of a good or bad experience that they have, and only if they know them.

Are women using social media to talk about YOUR company, its products, and its services? The answer is yes! A follow-up question is, "What are they saying?"

Let's look at one example: blogging. [93]

> **W** There are over 150 million blogs on the Internet.
>
> **W** Over 170,000 new blogs are being added daily.

Do blogs work? Are people actually reading the content? Well, numbers vary, but conservative estimates show that roughly one in five blog posts at any given time has something to do with buying a product or making a buying decision. More importantly, everyone has an opinion, and people are often inclined to accept as fact the opinion of another instead of searching for the truth themselves.

You'll notice that we're not having this discussion on social media in our marketing chapter, but in this stand-alone chapter on Company Reputation. While your marketing and communications departments certainly have a role, the broader context of your company's reputation must be managed in a more integrated and purposeful manner. It needs to contain the framework, strategies, and initiatives understood throughout your organization. This is important today given the immediacy of the message, the democratization of information, and the power of just one voice.

Given the ubiquity and high usage of social media, and a faster-than-lightning news cycle, it now takes no longer takes sixty seconds for news on an issue or challenge to circle the globe. Whether it is activist, investors, or perspective employees wanting to know more about your organization, there's a constant stream of data, chat rooms, comments, and articles on any given topic.

The speed of information, the connectivity of women, and the growing number of blogs and chat rooms are all compelling reasons for you to ensure that your Integrated Women's Leadership Reputation Strategy is formalized, integrated, and executed with the goal of program excellence. And you're not alone in this quest.

Your Competition May Already Have the Higher Ground

If you haven't already written and articulated a Women's Leadership Strategy, chances are you're a few steps behind your key competitors. As with all business initiatives, if your organization has not already stated its position or done something formally about it, they may already be playing catch-up. And when you're striving for "share of mind" in a highly connected world, being first and highly vocal is critical to being on top of the message and a leader in the marketplace.

- Do the vast sea of consumers and your actual customers really care if Procter & Gamble is ahead of Kraft on some diversity list? Do they care if ConAgra is even on the list?

- Will Deloitte and Accenture attract less consulting clients because they trail PWC in diversity programs and initiatives?

- Do the senior leadership teams at Hilton, Hyatt, and Starwood really care if Marriott is ahead of them on the list and has been so for the past five years?

The answer regarding ConAgra, Deloitte, and Accenture is YES. Though not as much in the public eye, companies in the B2B world do compete for female talent. They're aware that female college recruits are studying their company websites for signs of reputation. It makes a difference for companies like Walmart to win awards for "strongly encouraging" their partners and suppliers to bring more women to the table.

The answer for Hilton, Hyatt, Starwood, is a huge YES as well, primarily because of the heated competition for female consumers who influence over ninety percent of vacation decisions.

I don't know of many successful companies that are happy finishing second to anyone. Having fought in the Cola Wars for over twenty years, I can tell you,

Coke is happy any time it finishes ahead of Pepsi on any list and for any reason, and Pepsi is constantly seeking that same level of satisfaction!

Companies that have their finger on the pulse of the marketplace are in it for the win. They recognize the value of female talent at all levels in their organizations and the dominance of the female buyer across all categories in the marketplace. Internally and externally, they're executing their Integrated Women's Leadership Reputation Strategy and winning with women.

External Corporate Communications

Most Fortune 500 companies publish some sort of Corporate Citizenship materials. This work highlights many of the CSR elements already discussed. An increasing phenomenon is for companies to publish a diversity and inclusion report. These reports are valuable as they clearly state the connection of women/diversity to the organization. This external report is important and a standard best practice. If your organization is doing one it is already ahead of the curve. The next litmus test is, does your organization pass a simple "Content Connection Test?"

Conduct this experiment yourself. Visit your company's website home page. Typically, you will find a tab there that speaks to Diversity or Values, and as you click through, you'll most likely see pictures of happy people of many cultures, smiling and working together. Now return to your home page and click on the tab that introduces your executive leadership team. What do those faces look like? My guess is they look significantly different from the faces you saw on the diversity page.

Your corporate website speaks volumes to your commitment to winning with women. Do you have a "content disconnect" between your intent and your reality? A talented young woman graduating at the top of her class and seeking a place to build a career and move up into a leadership position has just left your website thinking,

"I clicked on the executive leadership team tab and didn't see anyone who looks like me. Why would I even consider working for that company? I wouldn't I have a snowball's chance in advancing there!"

This may seem like an obvious test and yet I cannot tell you how many companies fail. This simple test reinforces the critical need to have a truly integrated communications plan throughout your entire organization.

Summary Points from Chapter 8

- Your company reputation is under attack! While your marketing and communications departments certainly have a role, the broader context of your company's reputation must be managed in a more integrated and purposeful manner.

- This concept of trust lies at the very core of the company reputation connection. The lens applying this to women bring in the intersects of transparency, expertise, commitment, and empathy.

- Do not confuse empathy with sympathy. Empathy is the ability to mutually experience the thoughts, emotions, and direct experience of others and should not be confused with sympathy, which is a feeling of care and understanding for the suffering of others. Women do not want your sympathy but they do want your empathy.

- Organizations are connecting with the value of the Triple Bottom Line, focusing not solely on its finances, but giving consideration to the company's social, economic, and environmental impact.

- Your completion also wants to claim a leadership role with women so a sense of urgency is critical.

- Since women control 85 percent of the spending in this country, it's fair to say that at least 85 percent of your company reputation is in their heads and hands as well.

WHY WOMEN Readiness Assessment

1. How prepared is your senior leadership team for a public relations nightmare? Do they understand the need for expertise and empathy? Does your website communication pass the connection test of your senior leadership team matching the representation of your diversity pages?

2. Women are using social media to talk about your company and its products and services. What are they saying and what actions are they taking and are these positives or negatives? What are people saying on glassdoor.com about your company?

3. Chances are, your company is already doing something in regards to supporting women and communities through its philanthropic and CSR endeavors. Have you ensured that all of your efforts are connected back to your broader Integrated Women's Leadership Strategy?

Deepening Your Learning

— *Book* —

Reputation Rules: Strategies for Building Your Company's Most Valuable Asset, Dr. Daniel Diermeier

— *Online Article* —

"Leadership and the Triple Bottom Line," Center for Creative Leadership (2007)

— *Website* —

http://www.glassdoor.com

Part 3:

Realigning the Organization for Success

Chapter 9

The Need for Male Champions

"Regarding male engagement, they can't just show up and give a nice speech. They've got to be able to be seen as 365, 24-7, committed to inclusiveness, diversity, or a gender-related initiative in their organization, to really have the impact."

—Bob Moritz, U.S. Chairman of PricewaterhouseCoopers [94]

"You do what?"

I tend to draw this response when I tell friends, colleagues, or perspective clients what I do. My company, YWomen, focuses on engaging men in women's leadership development and the reactions are always interesting to hear and watch. Women will be genuinely interested, lean into the conversation, and want to know more.

"Why is a *man* doing this work?" "Do we really have an ally in him?"

When women ask me why I'm so focused on the advancement of women, I respond by saying,

> *You really don't need to convince women*
> *that we need to drive change;*
> *you need to convince men.*

Women's questions are not so much a sign of mistrust, although that sentiment may exist. I think it's more a surprise. Once they understand my work, they greet me like a best friend with smiles, the occasional hug, and sometimes, applause.

Men, on the other hand, react silently with a confused tilt of the head, a look of disbelief, and the unvoiced thought that I have sold out all men and will soon lose my membership to the men's club. Some men actually see my advocating for women as a betrayal of trust, an important tenet of the "man code."

Engaging male leaders as champions and advocates for women in leadership and including middle management in that quest are the keys to operationalizing your strategy. You can have all of your women's initiatives developed and ready to roll out, but if you don't have the buy-in of men and the commitment of middle management, your Integrated Women's Leadership Strategy will never get off the ground and become an operating norm for your company.

To get that buy-in requires an understanding of the "man code," and why advocating for women—or what many men mistakenly consider "advancing women over men"—is hard for many men to digest and support. Nevertheless, there are male leaders who truly understand and are walking the talk. In this chapter, I'll examine the key areas that are needed to engage men in the work of advancing your women strategies, specifically:

- Five Things Leaders need to do Every Day
- Getting Middle Management Commitment
- Cracking the "Man Code"
- Characteristics of Male Champions

Five Things Leaders need to do Every Day

Male champions are men who "get it." Earlier in the book, I called them "ready-now" men. As I noted, the number of men who are ready to be champions in your organization is about 20 percent and I believe the actual number may actually be higher. They see the economic value in the business case for gender diversity. They recognize that the complement of different perspectives ultimately brings greater innovation, higher levels of productivity, engaged employees, and a closer relationship with the marketplace.

I know many male leaders who can see the value and would become champions if they knew what to do. They know that cultural transformation doesn't happen overnight and that it has to start with someone taking that first step through their own behavior.

> *"Okay Jeff, you've convinced me. What do you want me to do differently? I can get on board with the strategy part and can understand the need to be present and vocal on the topic. But really, what do you want me to do differently, like every day, to*

demonstrate to my organization that things are different? What activities or behaviors should I include in my daily routine?

"And please, I just don't have any extra time to devote to doing one more thing such as supporting the company's Women's Leadership Strategy."

These are the questions and the honest, bottom-line statements I hear most often from men. While they can conceptualize an Integrated Women's Leadership Strategy, the challenge is in operationalizing it— the point where intent becomes action. These are the five things that leaders can do to demonstrate their commitment, none of which will tax a leader's or company's time and resources. Some of these have already been touched on, but for the sake of clarity and integration into your daily routines, here are the five ways leaders can demonstrate their commitment:

THE FIVE THINGS LEADERS NEED TO DO EVERY DAY

1. Talk about the business case – always.
2. Ask tough questions and hold people accountable.
3. Maniacally manage talent.
4. Deepen your cultural competency.
5. Be symbolic in your commitments.

1. Talk about the business case—always.

Assuming you've done the hard work to create the strategy and develop the initiatives, it's just as critical to talk about it as you would any other business imperative. Getting leaders grounded in the granular sound bites around that business strategy dismisses any conversation that otherwise portrays it as a "because corporate told us to do it" initiative. The number one way to operationalize your Women's Leadership Strategy is to discuss it in every staff meeting, operational review, or standard business process update.

What do these sound bites sound like? It comes right out of Chapter 2—Creating an Integrated Women's Leadership Framework. Here are two key messages that you have seen me state multiple times in the book:

> *"By acting on our Integrated Women's Leadership Strategy, we will grow revenue, improve operating profit, and enhance company reputation."*

> *"Our 80/80/80 foundational business case is critical to the success of our organization. Women represent 80+ percent of decision makers in our industry; women and minorities represent 80+ percent of our available talent pool; and our aspirational goal for employee engagement is 80+ percent."*

These are simple, crisp statements and tie directly to the business case. The key is to make the words your own for your organization and embed those messages and ideas into your daily work and processes.

2. Ask tough questions and hold people accountable.

Though we discussed this to a significant level in Chapter 7, the number one way to demonstrate commitment is to hold people accountable. This is true with every one of your business initiatives. As leaders, when you become more comfortable talking about the business case for women in leadership, you'll become much more fluid in your dialogue and in asking tough questions. You'll then be able to do what leaders do really well every day—hold people accountable. Foundational to that accountability is the Integrated Women's Leadership Scorecard that you created in Chapter 7.

The strategies and measures in this scorecard must be pushed down into the organization so that everyone, especially middle managers, are aware of their role and accountabilities.

As we've said before, if you're not tracking it, it can't be measured. More importantly, if you do create a scorecard that's left in a binder on a shelf in your office or just owned by someone in HR, the people in your organization will quickly gather that the scorecard is not relevant to their daily work. Employees may also become more critical and even cynical for the time they invested in activities and development and see nothing come of it.

It's critical for your scorecard to become a business initiative document that is regularly reviewed along with all your other business critical initiatives.

Talking about the business case and holding people accountable doesn't require any additional work on your part. These discussions and measurements are merely incorporated into your team's standard routines and processes. Talking up the business case and holding leaders and managers accountable will go a long way to ensuring your initiatives are operationalized.

3. Maniacally manage talent.

I choose the word manically very carefully. Manically means "characterized by ungovernable excitement or frenzy." [95] Do you have an ungovernable excitement about your best talent? The war for talent is real, and as we've said before, HR cannot have the sole ownership and responsibility for the talent in your organization; it must be owned by the field and frontline leaders across your operating units. People drive revenue, people drive engagement, and people drive your culture and company reputation.

> *Maniacally managing talent means that you are demonstrating real commitment and excitement to all the people who work for you—not just women.*

We all know that the number one reason people leave organizations is not because of compensation, too much travel, or the hard work itself. The chief reason is that they don't feel appreciated and valued, particularly by their immediate supervisor. It doesn't matter if this is an individual contributor to manager relationship, a manager to director relationship, or a director to vice president relationship. The need to feel valued, supported, and challenged are critical to the success of the organization.

Leaders today must understand that the key to getting the best out of every person is to treat each as an individual and in a respectful manner. The days of managing everyone with one broad-brush approach are over. In order to obtain the best results of every person on the team, leaders need to step up and understand each person's nuances, situations, and motivations. Maniacally managing talent is demonstrating a commitment to people at all levels of the organization.

4. Deepen your cultural competency.

This is often difficult for men to do. It requires personal growth, a desire to learn, and a willingness to demonstrate a little vulnerability. For many men, these are challenging new behaviors to adopt, however, it's critical in demonstrating your commitment to women.

Up until now, we've articulated many of the issues, obstacles, and challenges that women face in organizations—but these are really just the starting places for men looking to build their awareness of what women are facing and thinking.

> *If you really want to know what's on a woman's mind,*
> *all you need to do is ask her, but in a genuine way.*

Be prepared to listen and not interrupt. Don't swoop in with a justification for why things are the way they are or attempt to explain them away as "just company policy." Generously listen and ask questions.

An additional way to build your cultural competency with women is to follow-up on all of the **Deepening Your Learning** activities at the end of each chapter. These thirty references as well as bibliography in the back of this book will enable you to build an incredibly strong foundation.

Distribute these articles and topline studies in your staff meetings as conversation starters. The goal is to create dialogue, not to assess blame or infer who, or what, is right or wrong. Your team can find tremendous growth by sharing information. Make it a part of the next team meeting agenda to discuss new information and explore ways to link the learning to the team's work effort.

5. Be symbolic in your commitments.

Once you accomplish Steps 1 through 4, Step 5 becomes your graduation exercise. Part of being a leader sometimes means just showing up. As a leader, people watch and observe your every move. The more you say one thing and do another, the more you lose the trust and respect of your team. Similarly, if you're willing to walk the walk and show unwavering commitment, your team will get behind you and follow you anywhere.

What do symbolic commitments look like?

- Attend one of the events hosted by your women's BRG. I guarantee you will be one of the few men there and am certain you will feel a bit uncomfortable, but don't let that stop you. Just showing up and demonstrating a genuine, inquisitive nature and a true desire to learn more speaks volumes to your commitment to women.

- If you're a senior leader, I would encourage you to become an executive sponsor of a BRG. This commitment is a huge step from passive participation to visual advocacy.

- Another important commitment you can make is by becoming a mentor, or ideally an advocate or sponsor, for talented women in your organization. If you're in a large organization, you can volunteer to lead a mentoring circle where you would mentor five to ten women at once. This can provide a tremendous learning opportunity for you. The mentoring circle can become a personal focus group for you—a finger on the pulse of women's issues and challenges in your organization. It's also a great value to the women in the group to learn and grow by sharing with each other.

Getting Middle Management Buy-In

In many regards, middle management may be one of the most challenging places to be in an organization today. Most middle managers are constantly charged with unrelenting deadlines, back-to-back meetings, challenging customers, and an ever-increasing amount of responsibility often without any real authority. It all collides to create a perfect storm of stress and never-ending deadlines with fewer and fewer resources to accomplish the work.

Beginning in 2008, the amount of work for many managers has increased exponentially as organizations have gone through reorganizations and restructures, most ripping out layers of middle management. The span of control of one manager, which used to encompass five to eight subordinates, has since swelled to eighteen to twenty-four. [96]

The people have gone away, but the work hasn't.

In his article, "Hold The Applause: Gaining Middle Management Buy-in to The Success of Your Diversity Initiative," Barry Callender describes the four significant challenges that most organizations face with their mid-level managers. [97]

1. They have difficulty understanding their connection to and role in the organization's business case for diversity.

2. They've been asked to "do more with less" and don't feel they have time to make diversity a priority.

3. Many are often promoted into management for their technical proficiencies, not for their leadership skills and have received little managerial training.

4. They believe that diversity does not apply to them because their teams are already heterogeneous.

These are all very real-world challenges faced by organizations. If we step back and examine the five things described earlier that leaders need to do every day, we can successfully neutralize each of these challenges.

Most mid-level managers have difficulty understanding their connection to and their role in the organization's business case for gender diversity.

This is why it's critical that the business case becomes an ongoing discussion point embedded in all strategic meetings and operating norms. Being asked to do more with less and not having time is addressed by incorporating your Women's Leadership Strategy into your ongoing processes and asking for updates, just as you would require updates of any other business program.

The next two challenges for mid-level managers—not having adequate leadership skills and the belief that diversity doesn't apply to them because of the heterogeneous makeup of their teams does, in fact, require training and development to correct.

These two challenges connect back to deepening cultural competency and making symbolic commitments. Learning and development today does not require going to a classroom. Understanding gender dynamics and even how "sameness" shows up in teams that are homogenous—in optics only—can be learned and discussed in staff meeting discussions, webinars, and readings.

So we talked about what you as leaders need to do every day to operationalize your women's leadership initiatives and also how to get middle management's buy-in and practice.

Two key discussion points still remain, the challenges of breaking the "Man Code" and the characteristics of Male Champions.

Cracking the "Man Code"

Yes, the "man-code" does exist. For most men it starts early in life and is reinforced in literally every aspect of our upbringing. Family, social norms, and even the media conspire to determine what defines a man. Be competitive, win at all costs, and crush the opposing team are all mantras that most men grow up supporting. It is not surprising that when this mindset graduates from college the male brain is ready attuned to viewing business as combat.

As described early in my book, most corporate cultures today are, in fact, built on male norms. In most organizations, they've been the foundation of business for decades and are so deeply ingrained in our culture that they are hard to augment or change. Not only are these male-oriented practices, policies, and procedures embedded into the corporate culture, they are also embedded in the psyche of most men since childhood when they first learned to operate within the boundaries of manhood.

As you study these four male behaviors, you'll also recognize how they epitomize day-to-day life in the Field, putting an even finer point on the reality of life and careers on the front line and how challenging a place it is for women needing to find success in order to advance.

In *Engaging Men in Gender Initiatives: What Change Agents Need to Know,* Catalyst Research highlights four common masculine norms that are emphasized to varying degrees in North American and Western European societies and, as a result, define their resulting corporate cultures. [98]

These male norms, considered a badge of honor in sales, operations, and supply chain, are factors that, often unintentionally, hold women out of the C-suite.

"Avoid all things feminine"

This is perhaps a fundamental principle of masculinity—a rule that mandates that men should never be seen conforming to any feminine norms. If a man is judged as having acted in ways that are consistent with any or all of the norms prescribed for women—he will often experience criticism, ridicule, and rejection by other men. His status as a man may be called into question and the more traditional the culture, the more severe the backlash.

This "policing" often occurs within male peer groups beginning at an early age and continues into adulthood. It's a huge component of male corporate norms.

Derogatory words, such as "sissy," "wimp," and "whipped" are regularly used to label boys and men who are viewed as acting feminine, or even being willing to work for a woman. These words are often an effective deterrent against future violations of the male code. In business, these middle and high school terms are replaced with demeaning phrases such as, "grow a pair," "man up," or "put a skirt on."

"Be a winner"

This principle of the male code is all about the attainment of status and position power. It defines as "manly" any activity that increases one's wealth, social prestige, and power over others. Men gain the approval of others when they make their careers a priority and pursue occupations in corporate management or politics to increase their social and economic status. This norm of "winning above all" is seen as a revered model of behavior, and contributes to and reinforces common gender gaps in leadership all over the world. It's one of the underlying reasons why men are over-represented in jobs that command the highest salaries and unilateral decision-making power.

Men who pursue fields that offer fewer opportunities for status gains are far less likely to be admired, especially if those fields are judged as better suited for women and their occupations. This drop in admiration in organizations often happens when men, especially young men, move into staff positions versus leadership roles. Male friends and colleagues will sometimes taunt the guy with barbs such as, "The Field must have gotten too tough for you!" or "Punching out so soon?"

"Show no chinks in the armor"

Men should be tough in body and spirit and never back away from the threat of physical harm. Projecting this toughness requires that men suppress their emotions and not show fear, sadness, anxiety, or uncertainty. It's more socially expected for men to act detached, confident, certain, and focused. In a business setting, showing emotional toughness is often regarded as a key leadership attribute in men. Unfortunately the same is not true for women.

While men are often seen as "assertive" and "competent," women showing the same behavior are often labeled as "cold," "aggressive," or "a witch."

This clearly links back to the "double bind dilemma" that we explored earlier. This model of supporting aggressive male behaviors serves to reinforce male company norms. And these behaviors, when taken on by women, actually have the opposite effect.

"Be a man's man"

This rule is also known as being "one of the boys." It calls for men to comply with all the masculine norms and, in doing so, win the respect and admiration of other men and enjoy a special sense of camaraderie and rank. Additionally, and with few exceptions, a man's man is required to demonstrate that he prefers the company of men over the company of women. He must also participate in stereotypically masculine activities such as watching sports, drinking beer, or attending gentlemen's clubs. These activities not only serve as rituals that reinforce masculine norms, but also promote social ties and solidarity.

These activities, when part of the work relationship, serve to exclude women from mentoring, networking, and sponsorship opportunities.

So what's it all mean?

My goal is certainly not to defend these masculine norms but to put them on the table as talking points so you may begin to think about the challenges associated with getting men to become champions. While you read this list, you can probably think of literally hundreds of ways these norms plays themselves out in organizational culture, most all to the disenfranchisement of women.

I'm often asked the question,

"Does this mean that women have to act more like men?"

My response is always an emphatic "No, of course not!" However, I believe it's critical that we acknowledge how important it is for women to know the rules that typically govern the cultures of many companies which are often male norms.

I'm certain that many women reading this book are asking themselves the question,

"If male norms are in fact company norms, then is it even possible to find and engage true male champions?"

The answer and the number of men who are ready, willing, and able to ally with you may actually surprise you.

Engaging Men as Champions

Clearly not all men are ready to engage in this work. Yet, in my experience, up to 20 percent are actually "ready-now" and the real number may be as high 40 percent. Many simply need to be invited into the conversation. Most of the women I speak to find this number to be incredibly high. The truth is, male champions do exist, and their reasons for being champions are multi-dimensional. The challenge is to engage them in both head and heart discussions and match the criteria required to become a male champion with the mindset and motivations they already possess.

The motivations are:

- A deep understanding of the business case

- An overwhelming sense of fairness

- A nonbiased view of talent

- A personal connection

Up until now, I have attempted to frame all of the work involved regarding creating and supporting an Integrated Women's Leadership Strategy in business terms. This is the "head" piece for men and is the first criterion mentioned for many male champions. Given their left-brain tendencies, they need to feel fully aligned with the business case. And given male norms,

They need to feel comfortable that they are not engaging in some "feminine activity" but are in fact carrying out their company's business imperative.

Understanding the value of an Integrated Women's Leadership Strategy as a business driver is the first and strongest criterion for becoming a male champion.

The second is an overwhelming sense of fairness. We all know what this looks like in the workplace. If you ask your employees for whom they would most want to work out of all the managers they know, many will point out someone who reflects the attributes of a great manager—someone who understands how to motivate, lead, and empower people.

You probably already know who these people are, for they are at their core, fair and equitable leaders. They can't help but wear it on their sleeve and are of the smartest and most well-respected people that the organization has to offer.

> *Managers who are fair and balanced to their core are candidates who meet this second criterion for being a male champion.*

The third criterion is a non-biased view of talent. We all know leaders who are just great assessors and developers of talent regardless of their gender. Many of the women who have made the CEO list will say that a man, at some point in their career, chose to help support or mentor them. They will tell you it had absolutely nothing to do with them being women but had everything to do with talent and working for a man who recognized it and was willing to take a chance on them and their potential. Men are often promoted on potential, so it is expected that male champions will naturally embrace this criterion with women.

> *Male champions are ready and willing to promote women based on their potential.*

While the first three criteria speak to the "head" component, this final condition is totally "heart" driven: a personal connection, typically with a female family member, relative, or close friend who works in the business environment—someone men have witnessed as having issues and challenges in their career. This could be a mother, sister, or spouse. These male champions have seen firsthand the struggles of the most important people in their lives and want to help them because they genuinely care.

And while a mother, sister, or spouse may be a strong tipping point, I have found that,

Virtually 100 percent of male champions share a "singular reason" to advocate for women:

IT'S ABOUT THEIR DAUGHTERS!

I started this chapter with a question often asked me by my male friends and colleagues once I describe what it is I do for a living.

I then share how I've reflected on my fifteen years in this work and my personal epiphany:

I'm a young Boomer. My generation of men, by-and-large, strives to be good fathers. Though my family moved a lot to support my career, my personal goal in the face of all that upheaval was to raise strong self-sufficient children. I have two children, a boy and a girl. Quite frankly, I rarely worried about my son. But as a father, I worry every day about my daughter. I know what she's going to face in getting her career off the ground and advancing in a male-oriented organization.

My peer group and I encouraged our young daughters to pursue their first passions, whether in music, sports, or some other middle school or high school activity. We tell them that they can do anything they want to do with their lives—to pursue any dream. We ensure that they go to great schools and get a great education. We talk to them, coach them, and nurture them.

Then the day they graduate from college, we stop advocating for the most important person in our lives. Well, that support must continue!

My daughter is less likely to make the same amount of money coming out of school as my son will—even if she negotiates for it. My son and my daughter will both earn great degrees, from great schools, and yet when they enter the workplace I'm supposed to be satisfied that she's going to make $0.77 for every $1.00 my son is making, or my neighbor's son is making?

As a father, I need to be outraged by this inequity.

And as a business leader I need to realize that if I am not advocating for women in my workplace today then no one is going to advocate for my daughter ten years from now when she's faced with the same biases, challenges, inequities and, quite frankly, bullshit, that I see women put up with today.

After I tell this story to my male colleagues, many will invariably say, "It never really occurred to me to make that connection."

I know that the women leaders reading this book will find it incredulous that men don't make that connection. Unfortunately, it's true in most cases.

I worked in corporate America for almost thirty-five years and I now consult with Fortune 500 companies. I can attest that I have never found that smoke-filled room hidden deep in the bowels of an organization where men intentionally conspire together to hold women back. It just doesn't exist. What does exist is a mindset that produces a steady flow of unintended consequences.

I know for myself, that this was a huge blind spot for me for almost twenty years—even while I was mentoring women. I was not a sexist. I spoke of being fair and equitable, however, I never internalized this to arrive at that understanding the power and responsibility that men have, specifically those fathers of daughters who need to be their first male champion.

There's a famous quote by Madeleine Albright that fits well here: [99]

"There's a special place in hell for women who don't support other women."

I have a corollary to this.

I believe there is an extra special place in hell for those fathers of daughters, who, once they make the connection of the real issues facing women in the workplace, still choose to do nothing about it.

How powerful is male advocacy? If you examine most of the best practice companies that we've profiled and asked the male leaders that I've interviewed for this book, almost every one of them has at least one daughter. To take this one step farther, as a male leader of your organization ask yourself one simple question:

Would you want your daughter working for your company?

If your answer is yes, more power to you. You're probably a male champion and the opportunity now is to get more men in the boat with you. If your answer is no, I think you know you have a lot of work to do.

I mentioned that I believe that many men are ready and willing to help support women. This is not an easy task for them to undertake. To do so requires overcoming those challenging male norms that most men have been raised to follow. And though I dislike using the word "journey" when it comes to organizations, I believe it is entirely appropriate for individuals. This is, in fact, a journey—a journey of discovery for the vast majority of men.

Being a male champion is not something you become good at overnight. I can tell you though that men who embrace male advocacy and become male champions will at least be able to look their daughters in the eye and say, "Yes, I tried to do my part to make this a better world for you."

Summary Points from Chapter 9

- Engaging male leaders as champions and advocates for women in leadership and including middle management are the keys to operationalizing your Integrated Women's Leadership Strategy.

- These five steps of things leaders need to do every day: (1) always talking the business case, (2) holding people accountable, (3) being maniacal about managing your talent, (4) deepening your cultural competency, and (5) symbolizing your commitment, will enable even the toughest audience—your middle management—to understand the significance and importance of your women's initiative.

- You can have all of your women's initiatives ready to roll out, but if you don't have the buy-in and commitment of middle management, your strategy for winning with women will never become an operating norm for your company.

- The "Man Code" comprised of male cultural norms is real and must be discussed within organizations.

- Up to 20 percent of the men in your organization are "ready-now" to be male champions and have the attributes. Another 20 percent just need a little help. Men need to be invited into the conversation.

- The challenge is to engage them both in a head and heart discussion and match the four criteria required to become a male champion with the attributes they already possess.

- Understanding the value of an Integrated Women's Leadership Strategy, being a fair and equitable leader, and having a non-biased view of talent are the three "head" criteria for becoming a male champion.

- The final criterion is a personal connection, and for many men, that personal connection is with their daughters, understanding the challenges they will face in adapting to and advancing in a male model of business, and wanting to do something about it.

WHY WOMEN Readiness Assessment

1. Are you creating a culture that supports your Integrated Women's Leadership Strategy by talking about the business case daily, holding managers accountable, maniacally managing your talent, deepening your cultural competency, and displaying your own commitment? What steps are you taking to insure middle management ownership and engagement?

2. There are four male cultural norms that comprise "Man Code:" avoid all things feminine, be a winner, show no chinks in the armor, and be a man's man. How do they play themselves out in your organization and how are they inhibiting the growth of women (and male champions)?

3. If you are a father of a daughter, have you made the connection that by not advocating for women today that no one will be advocating for your daughter in the future? What actions are you prepared to take to become an advocate for women within your corporation?

Deepening Your Learning

— *Book* —

The Rise, Creativity, The Gift of Failure and the Search for Mastery, Sara Lewis

— *Online Article* —

"Engaging Men in Gender Initiative: What Change Agents Need to Know," Catalyst Research (May 2009)

— *Website* —

http://onthemarc.org/home

Chapter 10

The Unmentionables

"There are five things you never discuss at work: religion, politics, personal finances, your personal medical maladies, and your sex life."

—Monster.com [100]

I was attending a women's leadership conference a few years ago. The speaker, a renowned expert in women's leadership had finished her presentation and opened up the session for Q and A. In a room of about 300 women a lone man from about a handful of men in attendance walked up to the microphone and asked a simple question of the speaker. "Okay, you've convinced me, what is the one thing I should change in my organization?"

Before the speaker could respond a female senior executive in the audience stood up on the other side of the room and without hesitating, walked to the microphone nearest her and addressed the man saying, "All I want you to do is answer the question, 'why?' Why aren't there more women at the table? Why doesn't our talent pipeline resemble our marketplace? Why haven't you personally supported and sponsored women?"

These kinds of questions continued for several more minutes and the woman's tone became louder and increasingly confrontational. I can tell you that from my own experience, this man had summoned a lot of courage standing up like that and asking those questions in a room filled with women.

After receiving a bit of applause for her comments, the man, still standing at the other microphone paused for a moment then said,

"I will if you will."

His response caught the audience by surprise and many clapped in agreement. The women knew what he meant, and may even have recognized that deficit in their own behavior. They applauded him for calling it out. This was a watershed moment for the entire room and caused everyone to pause and reflect. Though rarely talked about, the issue of women supporting other women is certainly rarely talked about out loud in organizations.

In every organization there are topics we are afraid to discuss, especially regarding sensitive and contentious topics like gender, race, sexual harassment, and money. These "unmentionables" become additional derailers and roadblocks that will impede the progress that organizations are trying to make in implementing their Integrated Women's Leadership Strategies. Each chapter has highlighted some of the challenges that exist for women, revealing both the impediments and the solutions.

Yet there are a few final sensitive and unspoken corporate issues that arise, specifically the challenge of—women supporting other women, the unspoken issues between white women and women of color, the pervasiveness of sexual harassment, and several other "corporate unmentionables" that are rarely discussed in business settings.

Women Supporting Women

Up until now, I've talked about the importance of involving men in women's leadership issues. During my keynotes, I focus 100 percent of my time speaking to the business case, the importance of scorecards, and how to find and recruit male champions. Invariably, women will approach me afterwards and share their thoughts and personal situations with me:

- "I wish my female boss could have heard your presentation. Not only does she not support women, but I actually believe there's a higher standard that she holds women to."

- "I never got any help on my way up, why should I help someone else? I made it on my own and quite frankly the women under me should too."

- "I would like to help some of my female colleagues but I'm currently the only woman in a position of power. If I help them, the rest of the leadership team will think I'm playing favorites because I'm a woman."

All of these are very real concerns. Is there a double standard? Do women tend to hold their female peers and subordinates to a higher standard? Is there a penalty for supporting a woman when she's the only one on the team? Do women harbor animosity toward women being promoted when, for years, they themselves couldn't break through the glass ceiling?

Unfortunately, the answer to all of these is, "Yes."

Over years in leadership development, I've grown to realize that being a great leader has nothing to do with gender. Invariably, when I advocate moving more women into leadership roles, many women will say,

"I've worked for many women and they've all been horrible managers."

I will be the first to admit that there are many bad women managers in the workforce. I will also stipulate that there are many bad male managers. Being a good or bad manager has nothing to do with gender. There are simply just a lot of poorly or not sufficiently trained leaders and managers in the workplace.

I spend the majority of my time with middle and senior leadership who have an average fifteen to twenty years of work experience. When we explore the subject of great leadership in my workshops, I have them do the following exercise:

Think about all of the managers you've had in your lifetime. Now count on your right hand the number of really great leaders for whom you've enjoyed working.

On your left hand, count the bad leaders over the course of your career.

Typically, we can count the number of great leaders on one hand. On the other hand, many have lost count of the number of bad managers they've experienced over the course of their careers. After a brief back and forth on "why so many bad ones and so few great ones," I ask them one more question,

> ### *"If the direct reports you've managed over the years completed this exercise, which hand would you be on?"*

When I look across the audience after asking that question, I see some very sheepish faces. That being said, let's explore a little deeper into the claims that women make regarding women bosses and share some possible solutions to these derailers.

" . . . there's a higher standard that she holds women to."

Women leaders and managers often hold the women on their teams and throughout the organization to a higher standard. Part of that mindset is, "I earned it the hard way and you should too." And there are some who feel animosity toward other women who are moved up quickly, when they themselves had to claw their way up when there were hardly any women in the organization.

It reminds me of the discussion around the HR Paradox in Chapter 6. Recall, there are some managers who simply hold all of their employees to a high standard and seldom, if ever, promote anyone. And then there are many who rank all of their employees the same way—extremely high. While they may believe this is fair, this mindset fails to distinguish and promote the true performers.

With a strong performance management and accountability system in place, you can remove this subjectivity and look at all your talent in an objective way. By comparing and calibrating their ratings, female and male managers can better balance the challenge of holding the women on their teams to a higher standard. Rigorous processes and feedback mechanisms are important to control for any unconscious bias that may exist in both men and women.

Both female and male leaders, especially those in positions with bottom-line responsibility, need to examine the overwhelming business case for blended leadership and company reputation and realize that it's in their best interest to promote not just women, but all the best available talent.

" . . . they'll think I'm playing favorites just because I'm a woman."

This concern for showing favoritism is an unspoken advancement-derailer for many women who are working for a strong female leader. It also creates a dilemma for many women in leadership positions who may want to promote a woman worthy of promotion, but don't want the rest of the leadership team to think they're promoting her just because she's a woman. What they'll often do instead is make that rising star prove herself longer and harder than she would a male candidate to show there's no favoritism.

The solution for both sides of this coin is the same. Strong HR programs and processes must be in place to minimize subjectivity and allow the leader to feel confident and comfortable that she or he has made the best decision. It's also best practice to have a diverse slate of interviewers. Though this is often done just to ensure that women are on the interview panel, in this case, it would be beneficial to also having men on the panel to offer an unbiased view. That way, if a woman is selected as the candidate, then it's a promotion validated by male leaders during the process and puts the notion of favoritism to rest.

This concern for showing favoritism affects not just women, but also people of color.

Women and minorities who hold leadership positions may especially face a backlash if they work to promote diversity, according to a University of Colorado study.

According to David Hekman at the University of Colorado's Leeds School of Business, "Women can lean in and try to bridge the confidence gap all they want, but they're going to be penalized for advocating for other women, just like non-whites are." [101]

The survey included 362 executives (CEOs, vice presidents, and directors) from industries such as banking and consumer products.

- The study uncovered an inverse relationship between a female-executive's score for her "dedication to diversity" and her average performance rating as a leader. The more she advocated for diversity, the lower her performance rating.

- White male executives, on the other hand, actually got higher ratings in their performance review scores from showing their dedication to diversity.

Hekman believes the negative stereotyping is a result of self-interest. "People are perceived as selfish when they advocate for someone who looks like them, unless they're a white man. It could help to have a white male head up corporate diversity efforts."

The significance of these findings is real and cannot be ignored. Organizations must implement programs and processes to insure absolute fairness. In addition to rigorous talent processes, targeted focus groups, and discussing these topics with members from your Business Resource Groups are additional ways for unmentionables to be genuinely discussed and resolved.

Another evolving derailer that is rarely examined is the unintentional divide between white women and women of color.

White Women and Women of Color

Trudy Bourgeois, CEO of The Center for Workforce Excellence, is the co-author of the Network of Executive Women's Leadership report, *Tapestry, Leveraging the Rich Diversity of Women in Retail and Consumer Goods.* [102] Bourgeois summarized the report as follows,

> *"White women and women of color are having significantly different experiences in the workplace. While both are advancing at higher rates than in the past, white women appreciate diversity from a gender perspective but they are more like white men in not recognizing or even acknowledging racial or cultural differences."*

The report went on to highlight five key areas:

1. Multicultural women are significantly underrepresented in leadership. In traditional corporate hierarchies key multicultural women are not developed or even included in secession planning at the rate of white women.

2. Multicultural women's unique challenges are not being addressed. Multicultural women have different workplace experiences that combine their gender and race/ethnicity.

3. White women and multicultural women perceive the workplace differently. White women only see the similarities they have with multicultural women. Without recognizing other differences, white women may inadvertently be supporting the conditions that hold multicultural women back.

4. Most corporate cultures encourage "covering." Multicultural women feel pressure tied to certain aspects of their lives and are sometimes uncomfortable being authentic at work.

5. To compete effectively, companies must advance multicultural women leaders. All initiatives must include a scorecard for multiculturalism as well as gender.

I have worked with Trudy for years and I know her to be a huge champion for all women. She went on to say,

> *"The point of the research is not to assess blame but to begin a conversation that is inclusive of all women. White women need to understand the importance of a more inclusive conversation. They need to step up as sponsors as they are now the second largest dominant workforce group and they don't realize the power that they hold."* [103]

In an interview with another industry expert, Stacy Blake-Beard, formerly of Harvard and now a Professor of Management at the Simmons School of Management, acknowledges that both white women and women of color have opportunities for development in building partnerships. This is particularly true as it relates to mentoring, sponsorship, and providing feedback.

"There can sometimes be a hesitancy among white women to engage in challenging conversations, which results in protective hesitation; they may have some concerns about how feedback to a colleague across racial lines will be received. The flip side is that women of color sometimes engage in protective defensiveness and purposely do not reach out for feedback. These relationship dynamics obviously are not the case with all women, and protective hesitation and protective defensiveness are not limited to white women and black women. These complicated interactions show up in both men and women and in all races. At the core, both of these relationship dynamics reflect the core importance of trust. If I trust you as a leader and I believe you are genuine and have my best interest at heart then I will accept your feedback and proactively ask it." [104]

Bourgeois and Blake-Beard both acknowledged this topic is not getting enough discussion in corporate America and further acknowledged the critical need for both white women and women of color to collectively advance this dialogue. I would add that men also need to be a part of the conversation.

The Tapestry report highlighted six key areas in their agenda for corporate change. To champion and leverage cultural fluency to achieve multicultural women's leadership, organizations must:

1. Appoint and develop ambassadors of change to coach leaders in developing cultural fluency and awareness.

2. Reward mentoring and sponsorship as multicultural women trail white women in executive sponsorship.

3. Embrace and acknowledge differences in leadership styles.

4. Develop the pipeline through measures and metrics.

5. Create opportunities for multicultural women to be heard and recognized.

6. Measure multicultural performance, advancement, and retention.

The solution to the challenge, as in most issues involving cultural sensitivity, is to first seek to understand. Gender and race discussions often hold potential landmines for all parties involved. Having been a white male in this field, I've often found that if you are genuine in your intent and truly seek to understand the context and the issues of the person you're speaking with, a meaningful dialogue with ensue. You'll grow in your cultural understanding as a result of it.

Sexual Harassment

If you ask any woman who has spent any significant amount of time in sales, supply chain, operations, or a host of other areas that are dominated by men, they will tell you that sexual harassment just "comes with the job." Most women say that they just learn how to deal with it. Some shrug it off, some try to ignore it while it's happening, and others choose to address it head on.

All summed up how they dealt with (and for many, are still dealing with) that one particular challenge in a familiar but unfortunate phrase . . .

Don't Ask and Certainly Don't Tell

Whether it's playful banter, a stare that lasts a few seconds too long for comfort, a direct solicitation, or an outright sexist remark, sexual harassment whether intentional or not is quite prevalent in organizations. And it's not occasional for women, but rather a steady drip, drip, drip that's ever-present. Though sexual harassment can occur in any area of the business, I also believe that women in field roles are routinely subjected to this at a greater level. How prevalent is some form of sexual harassment in the Field?

Go and ask any of your female colleagues if they've ever experienced either verbal or physical sexual harassment My projection is that three out of five will say yes!

I know this will be a shocking number for you to digest. It is just one of the things that women have to deal with that we men don't talk about. Hard numbers for harassment in the field are tough to come by as many cases go unreported.

Your first inclination as men is to reason that harassment might have more occurrence as you work through the lower levels of the organization, down through to the manufacturing floor or warehouse. You'll assume that's where it mostly happens, where younger and less educated men might act unconsciously but more offensively to their women subordinates, peers, and even bosses.

If you ask women, it's actually just as common among senior leadership but it looks significantly different.

One woman I interviewed recalled something she experienced after her last executive committee meeting, when the team went out for dinner.

"We were all sitting in a special dining room next to the wine cellar in one of the most expensive restaurants in San Francisco. The CEO sat at the head of the table and the twelve of us, including three other women, sat around that huge table. An attractive waitress entered the room to take our drink order and took the CEO's drink order last. The room was silent for a moment as the waitress walked away, and we could all hear the CEO say in a just loud enough voice, 'Wow, I'd really love to nail that.' I'm sure the waitress heard him as well. Some of the other men at the table chuckled silently."

"Didn't he realize that there were women around the table? His response shocked my female colleagues and myself. How could he be so unaware? The funny part is, we know he is happily married and would not cheat on his wife. My guess is he may have made the comment to impress the men at the table. Sadly, we all have a lesser opinion of him now, regardless of what he says or does in the future."

Does this one comment make for a hostile workplace? Of course not, but it is exactly the type of thing that goes on literally every day. Most women ignore it, or chalk it up to "boys being boys."

Growing in importance in the workplace is also a trend related to harassment and that is bullying. A recent poll CNBC poll stated that,

> **W** Fifty-two percent of women report bullying or harassment of some kind. [105]

The study also acknowledged that the bullying of women wasn't always being perpetrated by male colleague, but was sometimes often female-on-female.

Sexual harassment and bullying is truly an organizational challenge and a major issue when you consider your talent pipeline and how you are setting up the women in your company to be successful. What's unfortunate is that this form of endless irritation for women is not only found in business but throughout most of their educational endeavors before even reaching the corporate world.

When we consider the need to recruit and retain women with expertise in science, technology, engineering, and math, the following research actually becomes quite alarming. [106]

> **W** Sixty-four percent of women in STEM experienced some form of sexual harassment.
>
> **W** Twenty percent have actually been victims of sexual assault.

In 2006, The Hidden Brain Drain, a task force comprised of forty-three global companies, surveyed the women in their ranks with degrees in science, engineering, and technology. Named *The Athena Factor*, this project set out to discover the career trajectories of these women. Their findings were even more startling.

Women represent 41 percent of highly qualified scientists, engineers, and technologists in middle management, yet 52 percent quit their jobs early in their careers for three recurring reasons—none related to job difficulty: [107]

> **W** Hostile cultures: Often exclusionary and predatory, 63 percent experienced sexual harassment.
>
> **W** Isolation: A woman can be the lone female on a team; 43 percent lack mentors and 83 percent lack sponsors.
>
> **W** Uncertain career paths: 40 percent feel stalled or stuck in their careers.

For most women—and regrettably long before that during their college years—"don't ask and certainly don't tell" is often their conclusion and the reality they accept for want of a career. For so many, it becomes just part of the game.

If you truly want to understand the challenges and dynamics including the subtle forms that sexual harassment and bullying can take, all you need do is ask the women in your organization.

I think you will be very, very disappointed in the responses that you get.

The Funding Fallacy

Another question I'm often asked as I speak to business leaders is, "How much money are other organizations investing in their women's leadership strategies?"

The answer will vary depending on the functional areas in the organization and their lines of sight:

HR professionals will often speak to costs associated with:

- Diversity training programs for employees

- Coaching and development of high-potential women

- Recruitment strategies

- Funding of Business Resource Groups (from small amounts all the way up to $25,000 per group per year)

- Industry conference events, summits, and seminars

Marketing professionals will often cite:

- Media spending

- Research and development

- Advertising and point-of-sale marketing collateral

- Packaging

- Responses to social media

Procurement will talk about the cost and resources associate with:

- Purchasing products and services through women and minority-owned businesses.

In researching best-in-class companies in diversity, you'll find that their funding of women's programs and initiatives typically falls into one of these three areas above. Don't be misled by the impact of elements under marketing and procurement. In B2C companies, the investment in those two areas alone can easily add up to hundreds of millions and even billions of dollars.

Yes, some companies are in fact making huge investments in women in HR, marketing, and procurement, but in reality, that's just part of their annual budgeting.

The challenge I find is with the exception of a handful.

__Most organizations cannot articulate the amount of incremental money they are spending on an Integrated Women's Leadership Strategy above and beyond their normal marketing and procurement expenditures.__

When you remove from the HR ledger the cost of "diversity training programs for all employees," the total incremental dollar amount allocated to women's initiatives is often well less than $1 million.

Given that most of the Fortune 500 generate billions of dollars in revenue each year, this makes the amount of money spent on women's initiatives a rounding error and not even an asterisk on the balance sheets of most annual reports.

Could the senior leadership of your organization identify how much and where the money is being spent? Does anyone know, or more importantly, does anyone care?

__The funding fallacy is that most companies are not investing any significant incremental dollars on a true Integrated Women's Leadership Strategy.__

My intent is not to minimize the dollars spent by HR, marketing, or procurement. However, if organizations truly felt that women were a top operating priority because of the huge profit potential, the money allocated would be in the hundreds of millions rather than in a rounding error that's less than $1 million.

One of the simplest methods for organizations is to have a dedicated individual or staff focused on their Integrated Women's Leadership Strategy. Most corporations today allocate a portion of someone's time while they maintain their full-time job responsibilities. This would be unheard of if you are launching $100 million initiative, and yet when it comes to companies demonstrating a true commitment to women this is often overlooked. Ask yourself this question as you look at your commitment to women:

How many full-time resources do I have dedicated to my women's leadership strategy?
My guess is the answer is none!

The funding fallacy and inadequate staffing against the opportunity are often hidden roadblocks for most companies that are never discussed. In fact, it is impossible to pinpoint and target total corporate spending on women. This is why it is so critical to operationalize, internalize, and scorecard every element of your integrated strategy.

The Benign Middle

I have already mentioned the importance of Middle Management. I stated that I believe up to 20 percent of men are ready and willing to support you in this work. This means there is a larger percentage that falls into the "benign middle"—those who do not have a strong point of view either way. For the sake of our discussion, let's call this 65 percent of the organization. This leaves 15 percent who may never get it and I will discuss those at the end of the chapter.

For the benign middle, these employees will often go with the flow, look at it as another corporate initiative, and choose to either moderately engage or just not rock the boat.

And while they may be neutral in their embracing the concept, many times the argument they'll pose is based on a common sense observation:

"It just doesn't seem fair that we promote women ahead of men. That just sounds like we're trying to meet a number or quota."

This of course, harkens back to everything we discussed in the book— they need to hear from their senior leadership that this is important. They need to know that the strategies exist and that their managers understand those strategies and can walk the talk. They need to see programs and processes that support fairness and equity. They need to understand that when a woman is promoted over a man, it's because she's better qualified and ready to take on the job. Finally they need to see transparency in organizational metrics. Only through a truly integrated business strategy will an organization be prepared to engage in this change. Demonstrating transparency in hiring, promotion, and advancement is the simplest way for everyone to understand what is going on in the organization. The simplest answer to this common sense question is to say,

"I know it may not sound fair but in fact men are still getting 75 percent of promotions in the company. If anything, our current model is a bit unfair to women."

Transparency and facts are the easiest way to deal with employees who do not have strong opinion one way or the other.

Sexists, Bigots, and Idiots

Finally, just as in society, every organization is filled with it's share of sexists, bigots, and flat-out idiots. The percentage in your company may be large or small, but you most likely know who they are through their past behavior. They represent an often-vocal small minority. This is certainly not to say they are just men, as women and minorities may also be sexist and bigots. We are, after all, human. A number of years ago, when I was delivering hundreds of hours of classroom diversity training,

I decided that I am not an idiot whisperer!

I arrived at the conclusion that some folks will never grasp the concept or importance of this work. Oftentimes, they are very vocal in the organization and my conclusion is you'll never be able to have a rational discussion or dialogue with your sexists, bigots, and idiots.

There's an old maxim that says, "You can't win an argument with an idiot," so my coaching to you is to not even try. You can say that, "This is the path the organization is choosing to take, and we are attempting to build a much fairer and equitable company for all associates."

As with all organizational initiatives, you can certainly choose to not engage in or support them. If you in fact choose not to support them, then this may no longer be the right company for you. While my belief is that you will not change their mindset or their point of view, your declaration usually causes even the most vocal and self-righteous idiot to pause for a moment. Whether they choose to acknowledge it or not, chances are, if your organization is serious in its commitment, these individuals will choose to leave on their own accord.

Given everything we've talked about, the business case for change, the new face of talent entering your organization, and the complexity of work today, if you truly implement an Integrated Women's Leadership Strategy, sooner or later, the sexists, bigots, and idiots will figure out the need to go and find the door on their own.

It is time for organizations to get used to the conversation; it is not going away anytime soon.

Summary Points from Chapter 10

- The key to creating an effective Integrated Women's Leadership Strategy is to acknowledge that there are sensitive and unspoken corporate challenges that are hindering progress.

- Women will often say, I've worked for a number of women managers and none of them are very good. Being a good or bad manager has nothing to do with gender. There are simply just a lot of badly trained leaders and managers in the workplace.

- Women leaders and managers often hold the women on their teams and in their organizations to a higher standard. Part of that mindset is, "I earned it the hard way and you should too." And there are some who feel animosity if other women are move up quickly, when they themselves had to work their way up when there were hardly any women in the organization. These are real issues and must be discussed.

- White women and women of color are having uniquely different experiences in the workplace. White women need to look beyond gender as their diversity lens and include multiculturalism as a key component.

- Sexual harassment and bullying is a very current and real problem in organizations. While the issue is present in all levels of the organization, it can be particularly hard for women in the field who feel isolated and alone.

- Research shows that sexual harassment particular in STEM begins to show itself as early as undergraduate work. This is a contributing factor to women opting out of STEM careers.

- A funding fallacy exists in organizations as few incremental dollars are allocated for their women's leadership strategy. This is demonstrated a lack of the ability for leaders to quickly articulate what the company is doing as well as lack of full-time staffing around the opportunity.

- One of the keys to middle management buy-in is a transparency in the numbers of who is getting ahead in the organization. While many feel that women are getting ahead at the expense of men, the reality is the overwhelming majority of promotions and advancements is still going to men.

- Not everyone in your organization is prepared to think differently regarding women. You will never convert sexists, idiots, and bigots.

WHY WOMEN Readiness Assessment

1. Do women in your organization hold other women to higher standards, and have you engaged in a discussion around the challenges and sensitivities that may arise between white women and women of color?

2. Sexual harassment and bullying is a real concern for organizations yet it is rarely talked about or discussed. Is your organization conducting focus groups, feedback sessions, and training sessions to discuss the impact of sexual harassment and bullying and the impact it is having on your organization?

3. Can your organization and its leaders articulate, in financial terms, what the investment is in the company's Integrated Women's Leadership Strategy? If women are truly a priority, how are you staffing against opportunity? Is this a part-time responsibility or do you have full-time dedicated staff as you would with any other business imperative?

Deepening Your Learning

— *Book* —

In the Company of Women: Indirect Aggression Among Women: Why We Hurt Each Other and How to Stop, by Pat Heim

— *Online Article* —

"The Athena Factor: Reversing the Brain Drain in Science, Engineering, and Technology," *HBR* (June 2008)

— *Website* —

http://www.catalyst.org/knowledge/sex-discrimination

Summary

The RAVING CAPITALIST
Action Plan

"Mastery is not merely a commitment to a goal, but a curved-line, constant pursuit."

— Sara Lewis, *The Rise, Creativity, The Gift of Failure, and the Search for Mastery* [108]

As I meet and speak with women leaders and managers, there is always one unavoidable question that surfaces early in our work . . .

"Why is progress still so slow?"

The one-word answer is complexity. If this were easy work, we would have already made significant progress decades ago. Organizational cultures are often so deeply rooted that it may take generations of leaders to affect true change. The challenge for leaders today is to understand the totality and interdependencies required to be successful in building an integrated strategy. Every function from marketing, to sales operations and supply chain, to human resources requires

> *that middle management and senior leadership—at all levels—be in alignment and held accountable to real metrics.*

This is why organizations must move to an Integrated Women's Leadership Strategy. It helps to sharpen focus, drive accountability, and link the entire organization to the bottom line with a sense of urgency.

If you have worked the math and answered the questions throughout the book you already have the information you need. The challenge is to take this very complex topic and break it into elements that can be easily implemented in your organization.

The RAVING CAPITALIST Action Plan

Everything that has been covered in the book falls into one of the five categories of that were detailed in Chapter 9, The Five Things Leaders Need to do Every Day.

If you recall I am not asking you to do one more new thing. These are elements of work that every leader does every day. As you build your Action Plan step by step,

I want your frame of reference to always be, how is this making more money for the organization?

That is the RAVING CAPTIALIST part of the Action Plan.

Properly done, all of the elements below must link directly to a financial return for your company. Each day begins with every level and area of the organization understanding and appreciating the bottom-line value of a Women's Leadership Strategy.

THE FIVE THINGS LEADERS NEED TO DO EVERY DAY

1. Talk about the business case - always	• Chapter 2 - Create an Integrated Women's Leadership Framework • Chapter 3 - Develop your 80/80/80 Business Case • Chapter 8 - Manage your Company Reputation through an Integrated Communications Plan
2. Ask tough questions and hold people accountable	• Chapter 4 - Insure Sales and Marketing are measured and accountable • Chapter 7 - The Leadership Imperative for ownership, scorecarding, and metrics
3. Maniacally manage talent	• Chapter 5 - Understand the challenges and issues present in the Field • Chapter 6 - Discuss and resolve the series of HR Paradoxes that compound to hold women back
4. Deepen your cultural competency	• Chapter 10 - Begin a dialogue to truly understand the Unspoken Impediments that women face in your organization
5. Be symbolic in your commitments	• Chapter 9 - Engage Male Champions

Getting Started - Start Small

The final solution I would offer for organizations is to start small. You don't have to embark on major organizational changes around women. Find a department, a division, or an operating unit to test and operationalize your Integrated Women's Leadership Strategy. Most successful practices in companies start out small. I would encourage you to approach your Integrated Women's Leadership Strategy in the same manner. Too often initiatives fail because "everyone needs to be on board," and I can attest that when it comes to an Integrated Women's Leadership Strategy, that will never happen.

Find a single divisional president who is passionate and supportive of the work and is willing to test new programs, processes, and accountability methods. If it's successful, other divisions will quickly want to replicate the practices. To start building a plan simply figure out the business case in your division and in your words and begin to set metrics on revenue, talent, and engagement. Develop talking points that everyone understands and embraces.

Have set metrics, begin to talk about their progress in staff meetings, and ask tough questions as to why progress is not being made. Have deep meaningful conversations about talent. Conduct focus groups of your male and female employees and find out what is really on their minds. Create a safe place to bring up issues and express honest opinions such as a "lunch with leader" discussion group. Most importantly, lead from the front. Demonstrate your passion, your commitment, and a sense of urgency. As you formulate your plan quick wins become critically important to demonstrating commitment and celebrating success.

One Quick Win

I'm often asked is there one quick next step an organization can do to immediately demonstrate its commitment to retaining and advancing women. The overwhelming response from all of the women I talk to is *flexibility*.

Work today is no longer a "9-to-5" activity, but a seemingly endless twelve- to fourteen-hour day that begins with checking emails during your morning treadmill, holding conference calls during your commute to and from work, and the endless stream of your many other business and family obligations.

When women were surveyed and asked the following question:

If you could have one of the following which would you pick?

- A promotion
- A raise
- Another week of vacation
- Flexibility in your day

The overwhelming response was flexibility during the day!

Seventy-five percent of college-educated women aged thirty-five to sixty would rather have more free time in their lives than make more money at their jobs. [109]

In fact, 40 percent would even take a pay cut for more flexibility.

While you would expect mothers to lean more heavily toward flexible workplace options so that they could spend more time with their children, 68 percent of women *without* children also said they would rather have more free time than more money.

In fact, they mentioned that they didn't even need flexibility for the entire day, just the hours between 4:00 p.m. and 7:00 p.m. Many of the women surveyed said if the company was willing to give them the flexibility they would actually be more than willing to get on their computers and work from 8 o'clock at night to 10 o'clock at night to make up for the time and work.

This one simple solution can serve to drive engagement and productivity for many of your workers, especially women. With today's weak economy and high unemployment rate, 33 percent of women believe it's career suicide to ask for more flexibility. While that number is still a little high, it means that the remaining 67 percent believe a balance between work and life is possible. [110]

Increasingly more organizations are providing the flexibility women (and men) are seeking. This makes sense, especially if companies want to retain all of their talented professionals. Of those surveyed, 42 percent said they would consider owning their own business to achieve that flexibility.

Where there's smoke, there's fire, and chances are that the most industrious and ambitious of your employees are in that four-out-of-ten group. The goal of any organization should be to keep the best on their team.

Taking the Next Big Step

Why Women: The Leadership Imperative to Advancing Women and Engaging Men is written to help you jumpstart your five- to seven-year strategic plan. When you are ready to move to the next level, look for high impact programming.

The *Wall Street Journal* published a special report on Women in The Economy titled "A Blueprint for Change" that pulled together 170 leaders of business, education, media, and government. To summarize their top five recommendations specifically targeted to advancing women in the organization: [111]

- **P&L leadership** - company should establish programs to train and encourage women to take leadership positions that involve profit and loss expertise, and develop plans to enable them to transition into these roles.

- **Leverage C-suite power** - holding the CEO accountable for hiring women in top jobs of equal pay. Use metrics and scorecards to track women's promotions in positions and if women are not promoted explain why not. Require diverse slate of candidates for high-level jobs. Expect a balance of men and women at the decision-making table.

- **Promote women on potential** - women should be equally considered for promotion on their potential as are men. Companies need to identify talented women early and nurture them. Employers should create incentives for female sponsorship, tying success mechanisms with compensation.

- **Mentors and sponsors** - develop more industry-wide and company-specific programs for both mentorship and sponsorship. Such programming should include secession planning and co-mentoring which allows advice to flow from junior to senior levels.

- **Strong talent management programs** - recruit outside normal channels and leverage diverse networks. Take risks on high potential women by rotating them through different positions and giving them exposure to senior leadership. Provide training in communications and strategic thinking.

Each of these five elements is critical to building a women's pipeline to leadership and keeping your best and brightest in your organization. My recommendation is that each be a key focus of your Integrated Women's Leadership Strategy.

Taking the Final Step

It is now time for action. Bob Moritz, U.S. Chairman of PricewaterhouseCoopers is a passionate man of action and a role model for all CEOs—male and female—who are looking to attract and retain the best talent. In a recent *Forbes* interview Moritz was asked, "What do you think are the biggest challenges for CEOs, male and female, to create this type of change in their organization?"

To summarize his response:

> *"The biggest challenge for any organization, regardless if led by a woman or a man, is to role model this. It takes personal time and energy; it takes continuous commitment; a self-assessment every so often to say, "Are you doing enough? And is there more that could be done?" So, creating the right tone at the top by the behaviors, not*

the words, is super important. Second, you've got to create the right culture and environment to make this cascade through the entire organization. You've got to set the expectation for the entire organization, get that accountability right, and cascade it through the leadership team. Third, you do need to put programs and initiatives in place. If you're going to be disruptive, the reality is, the natural biases, preferences, conscious or unconscious, are there. And there's got to be a counterforce to them to make sure that whatever you are doing doesn't end up producing the same results."

"And, last but not least, I think you do have to assist people – and this is leadership. And I'm going to use a small "l," not a capital "L." Leadership is defined as everybody in a position to lead, regardless of title, to behave in a better way. So you need to help coach them; you need to create that awareness. You need to give them the tools and techniques so they're doing the same self-assessment that the CEO should be doing as well, with the idea that, they, themselves, can continuously improve on this process. And then, assist the individuals in the organization to make their personal aspirations and provide the space and support to make the difference." [112]

The rest of the organization's plan is up to you. My hope is that I've provided you a strong foundation if you're just starting your Integrated Women's Leadership Strategy. If you are already well on your way, I hope that I've given you some new discussion points to jumpstart your initiative and accelerate it to even greater heights.

This book does not provide all the answers. My hope is that it raises more questions and generates more dialogue. It is only through leaders, men and women coming together and talking about the unique strengths of both genders, that we can be successful in truly understanding and unleashing the power of women in organizations.

Your Future RAVING CAPITALIST Action Plan

I ended Chapter 1 by saying there is a "the tsunami of change on the horizon is coming and it's called Women!" One book cannot encompass the totality of the change and the impact that women will be having in the next ten years, not just domestically, but on a global basis. While I believe women will still be at the center of the conversation, multiculturalism and millennials will change the dialogue even more significantly. As you look to build your future RAVING CAPITALIST Action Plan, here are some additional areas of dialogue that should be examined.

Workplace 2020

By 2020, the workplace will look significantly different than it does today. Millennials who are just reaching their early 30s will be well entrenched in middle and rising senior leadership. The way they work their use of technology and their unwillingness to accept status quo and to challenge authority will be completely manifest in the next five years. Jeanne C. Meister and Kerry Willyerd in their book, *The 2020 Workplace,* highlight ten forces shaping the future workforce now: [113]

1. Shifting workforce demographics. Twenty percent of your workforce will be fifty-five or older, and 47 percent of your workforce will be under the age forty-five.

2. The knowledge economy. Seventy percent of all U.S. jobs created since 1998 require a set of conceptual tacit skills and that number will continue to grow.

3. Globalization. The world is flat and becoming flatter. This includes tapping into a global talent pool and managing a virtual workforce.

4. The digital workplace. Organizations and workers will share work and information at escalating pace. The need to manage the security of data with employee access will become a critical organizational function.

5. The ubiquity of mobile technology. Mobile handheld devices and voice-to-voice technology will escalate the mobile phone is your most critical business and learning platform.

6. A culture of connectivity. Hyper connected individuals will blend their work and life culture representing an increasingly blurred lines between work and family and friends.

7. The participation society. Collaboration and knowledge sharing as individuals come together and solve corporate issues in a more collective manner.

8. Social learning. Learning that is collaborative, immediate, relevant, and presented in a content of an individual's unique work environment.

9. Corporate social responsibility. In the future companies will be judged and held accountable for their global citizenship and political and economic footprint.

10. Millennials in the workplace. Millennials crave freedom of choice and freedom of expression, look for corporate integrity and openness, and want to find entertainment in their work, education, and social lives. They thrive on collaboration and relationship building.

If we examine this list of workplace trends occurring in just a few short years against the topics described in our first ten chapters, we see women at the intersect of a multitude of these trends. The need for knowledge economy, a blending of work and life culture, and corporate social responsibility call for a new set of leadership skills that some would say are inherently female in nature.

Embracing Feminine Leadership Principles

In *The Athena Doctrine: How Women (and the Men Who Think Like Them) Will Rule the Future*, John Gerzema surveyed 64,000 globally, and two-thirds feel the world would be a better place if men thought more like women. [114]

Drawing from interviews at innovative organizations in eighteen nations and at Fortune 500 boardrooms, Gerzema reveals how men and women alike are recognizing significant value in traits commonly associated with women. His work is built on identifying the words associated with the leadership behaviors needed to be successful in today's organizations and then asking respondents to place a gender on those words. Increasing the words of twenty-first century leadership include nurturing, listening, collaborating, and sharing. Respondents typically would say these words are "feminine" in nature.

Here's how Gerzema speaks to that research:

> *"In the new economy 'winning' is becoming a group construct. Masculine traits like aggression and independence trail the feminine values of collaboration and sharing credit. Being loyal (which is feminine) is more valued than being proud (which is masculine),*

which points to being devoted to the cause rather than one's self."
He goes on to say, "We are wanting our leaders to be more
intuitive, (also feminine in nature). This speaks to the lack of many
leaders to have the capacity to relate to ordinary people and their
points of view."

In addition, Gerzema points out the traits associated with femininity underpin change management, career mobility, and even personal fulfillment. This is an interesting construct as we examine these findings across the *Workplace 2020* research. Clearly, the new elements of leadership for the twenty-first century will focus on connectivity, collaboration, and a deep cultural awareness of how to get the best work out of every employee. If these are in fact labeled "feminine traits" by 64,000 people globally, then the topic certainly deserves further dialogue in organizations.

Both *The Athena Doctrine* and *Workplace 2020* discuss the significance of having a global point of view. This represents a third area that cannot be ignored when it comes to women.

Global Women - An Evolving Discussion

Though *Why Women, The Leadership Imperative to Advancing Women and Engaging Men* is a business book largely based on research and insights of U.S. companies, the principles of an Integrated Women's Leadership Strategy are entirely applicable for any company in any country.

If I added 500 pages to the book, I could not begin to discuss the state of women globally. While some countries are embracing women in leadership, both in the public and private sector, other countries still treat women as second-class citizens. The challenge comes in trying to separate the working roles of women from the private lives of women.

Today, women represent about 50 percent of our worldwide population, but they do not yet receive 50 percent of the opportunities. Each year since 2006, the World Economic Forum releases its annual *Global Gender Gap Report*, which "examines the gap between men and women in four fundamental categories: Economic Participation and Opportunity, Educational Attainment, Health and Survival, and Political Empowerment." Out of the 110 countries that have been included in every report since the initial report in 2006, ninety-five have shown improvement over the last four years. [115]

The top countries for women are Iceland and the Scandinavian countries. In Iceland, there are over 1.5 women for every man in post-secondary education. In Norway since 2008, the boards of all publicly listed countries have been required to have 40 percent of each gender. And in Sweden, 44 percent of parliament is made up of women.

On the other side of the coin, countries such as Japan and India, and many in the Middle East are facing talent shortfalls. Young women in these and many other countries and regions of the world are pursuing college degrees in record numbers, yet are not being integrated into business and government. Many countries are slowly coming to realize the talent for the resources they need is within their own nations.

Government and Business Partnering

In late 2014, the state of Massachusetts launched a campaign to help organizations become more engaged in closing the gender pay equity at work. The "Getting to More" corporate challenge is among the first of its kind in the nation. [116]

Rather than mandating or legislating corporate policy, the corporate challenge is entirely a volunteer one. The goal is simple: enlist businesses to commit formally to grow and retain women at all levels, including board positions.

Businesses that commit to The Challenge can choose one (or more) of the following areas to focus on:

- Actively recruit women to fill open positions at all levels of the organization, in order to increase the percentage of women in the workforce, including non-traditional roles.

- Increase the retention rate of women at all levels of the organization.

- Increase the percentage of women among the top 10 percent of the company's senior positions.

- Increase the number of women on the board of directors.

- Monitor pay by gender and address such gaps as are discovered.

By participating in the challenge, companies are merely committing to making progress on what "Getting to More" means most to a business. Internal data and measurement related to the goal remains private unless a company chooses to release it.

"Women make up nearly half of the Massachusetts workforce and nationally they are the sole or primary source of income in 40 percent of households with children under the age of eighteen," said Gov. Deval Patrick. "If the Massachusetts economy is going to continue to thrive, employers must design a workplace that maximizes their talent and potential by eliminating the wage gap and focusing on family oriented practices and benefits."

I believe as we move forward in our discussion on advancing women we are going to see an ongoing trend in government and business policies that look to solve not just systemic issues in the workplace but in the economy as a whole.

Mounting Pressures for Change at the Board Level

Chances are, if you're reading this book, no one is coming to ask you for advice and input regarding the makeup of your board of directors. That being said, you must be aware of the facts and data and how this one element is on a list of many of what successful companies are doing.

The need for board diversity is well documented and numerous reports articulate the real bottom-line value of companies that have greater diversity of membership among its board of directors. The numbers and the results are very real. [117]

> **W** Return on Equity: On average, companies with the highest percentages of women board members outperformed those with the least by 53 percent.
>
> **W** Return on Sales: On average, companies with the highest percentages of women board members outperformed those with the least by 42 percent.
>
> **W** Return on Invested Capital: On average, companies with the highest percentages of women board members outperformed those with the least by 66 percent.

Current research at the board level that studies the dynamics of the discussion and the quality of decision making when women are present shows how the range of issues raised and discussed increases and includes different perspectives when female board members are involved.

This research shows that boards that contain women are more likely to pursue best practices in areas including board evaluations, codes of conduct, and conflict of interest guidelines, and look more closely at executive remuneration arrangements—all areas that help shape company culture.

The reason women make a powerful difference in the boardroom often ties back to the collaborative leadership style they bring. Their style benefits board dynamics by encouraging people to show up, listen more carefully, and focus on win-win problem solving. Also at this level, women are more likely to ask the tough questions and request direct, detailed answers.

Still, women's representation on boards is growing at a snail's pace, even given the endless number of studies that prove that the presence of women in leadership improves the performance of the organization. Given mounting media pressure and advocate shareowners the dialogue around this topic is only going to continue to expand.

Powerful Women versus Empowerment of Women

Maria Reitan is the president and chief strategy officer of Lola Red, a Minneapolis based PR agency. Maria is also host of *Purse Strings*, a Webmaster Radio show focused on women in business. Maria has had the opportunity to interview over 800 women and men in the past few years and I asked her what trends she sees evolving for women. [118]

> *"The change I'm seeing is around female empowerment. There is a feeling from women leaders that it's time we take the bull by the horns because we can't sit around and wait for organizations to do it. This is not just in organizations but within the broader marketplace as well."*

Maria referenced two recent examples. Women Moving Millions is a campaign created as a global contagion of committed, purposeful women making unprecedented gifts of $1 million or more for the advancement of women and girls. Women can commit their gift to any organization they wish, provided the mission is focused on advancing women and girls. In five years, they've raised over $500 million. [119]

Maria also referenced Sallie Krawcheck's organization, Ellevate (formerly 85 Broads) that is teaming up with Pax World Management, a fund management company, to offer an index fund focused on companies where women make up a significant portion of officers and directors. The top holdings include PepsiCo, where Indra K. Nooyi is the chairman and chief executive, and Lockheed Martin, where women make up a third of the board. [120]

> *"These are just two recent examples of things happening around the globe that reinforce the belief of women that I believe in myself, and that together with other women we can get this job done. We are sick and tired of waiting for men (and organizations) to fix the problem. Women are finally saying we can do it if we do it together."*

This collective coming together of women can also be redefined as women realizing the power that they have and taking control of that power. Carol Evans, CEO of Working Mothers Media frames it this way:

> *"We are seeing women standing up for other women. Women are feeling much more comfortable and confident in their own power. Finally I am seeing women, women very senior in their career who had previously not advocated for women realizing their responsibility to reach back in support women, even if they weren't supported. It is a very powerful time for women."* [121]

Wrapping up this research, I mentioned it to a female colleague, to which she replied, "This is certainly important work but I believe we need to stop talking about empowerment and just talk about the power of women. Women don't need to be empowered, we are already empowered."

All are strong points of view. Whether we are talking about empowering women or the power of women, we really need to move this conversation beyond semantics and focus on the change that is coming.

Why Women? Why Women! Why Women$

In summarizing the book, I am often asked why there is no question mark at the end of *Why Women*. Because *Why Women* is not a question but a statement of fact that should end in an exclamation point! Additionally it if were grammatically correct, I would also consider placing a $ at the end.

As I stated in my first pages, my goal is for you to read this book and make more money—for yourself and your organization. This cannot be done without a strong business rationale, a sense of urgency, solid metrics, and deep conversations around how to drive change. And while one of the premises of this book is the need to engage male leaders, I am hoping an outcrop will also be for women to understand the collective power that they currently hold.

Rather than arguing if Sheryl Sandberg is correct in espousing women to *Lean In*, [122] or Katty Kay and Claire Shipman in the *The Confidence Code* [123] are correct in suggesting that women need to be more self-assured, women need to stop arguing with other women and embrace their collective power.

Anne-Marie Slaughter, wrote a ground-breaking article in the *Atlantic* Magazine, "Why Women Still Can't Have It All." At the time a Professor of Politics and International Affairs at Princeton, Slaughter received thousands of emails and comments on the fact that she had by and large sold out all women. While clearly not the intent of the article, people's reactions were largely negative and those of condescension. [124] This was one powerful women stating her point of view and how it wasn't working for her. Though she stated that multiple times in the article it was lost in the rhetoric of her choice.

If I have learned one thing in the last fifteen years of doing this work, true progress will never come until women stop judging other women. Sheryl is right, and Katty and Claire are right, and Anne-Marie is right.

There is no one simple answer. The answer is as individual and unique as the tens of millions of women who are occupying the workplace today. The day that women realize that they are all in this together and see the collective power in bringing their voices together into unified goal is the day it will be game, set, match-over . . . and women and organizations (and a few men) will be the true winners.

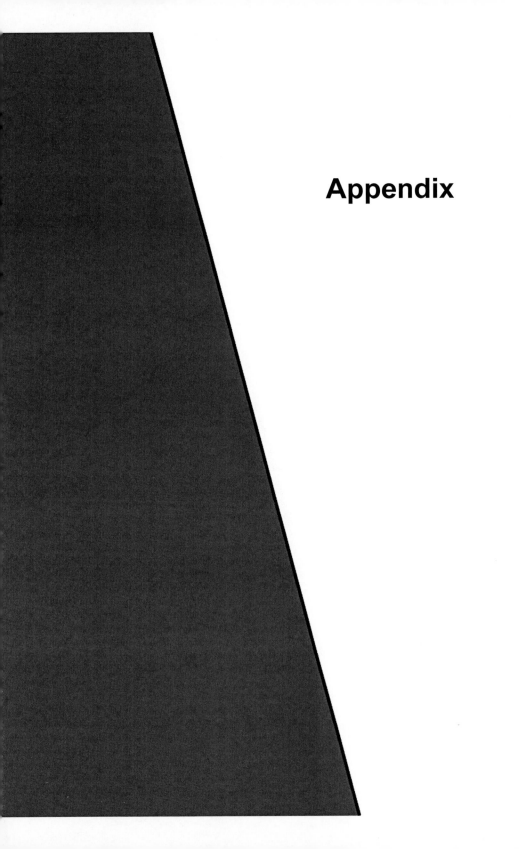

Appendix

Women's Leadership Measures and Metrics

YWomen Leadership Measures/Metrics

The Following Should Be Measured and Tracked for Every Functional Area of the Company

Talent: Current Baseline of Employees by Level, Sourcing Goals and Strategies, Percentage of Diverse Slates/Interview, Percentage of Diverse Panels/Interviews, Advancement Rates/Goals, Regrettable Loses, Tracking and Development of Hi-Po Talent, Formal Succession Planning

Engagement: Participation Rates, Engagement Levels by Age/Function/Tenure/Organizational Level, 360 Feedback, Step Level Interviews, Focus Groups/Feedback/Actions Taken

Area	Measures/Metrics (Develop Gender Baseline, Set Target)
Marketing	
Brand	Total/By Gender: Brand Awareness and Recognition, Brand Image/Health (Perceived Quality, Relevance, Credibility, Preference, Consideration, Purchase Intent), Consumer Behavior (Loyalty, Advocacy)
Media/Digital Media	Total Rating Points/Frequency/Reach vs. Target, Total Visits, New vs. Repeat Visits, Traffic Sources (Organic, Direct, Referral), Leads, Impressions, Conversation by Traffic Source
Innovation	Research and Development Dollars Focused on New Female Targets/Demos, Number New Products in Pipeline/Test Market
Agency	Representation of Agency by Function, Dollars spend with Women Owned Business Agencies, Agency Procurement/Spend by Vendor
Sales/The Field	
Market Share (Syndicated/External)	Share by Brand, by Market, by Customer, by Package, by Age/Demo, by Gender and Ethnicity
Baseline Business Performance (Internal)	Revenue by Segment/Channel, Opportunity Gap, Customer Analysis (Top 100) ROI, Profit Margin, Share of Wallet, Price Premium, Purchase Frequency, Purchase Conversion, Retention
New Business	Opportunity Gap for New Customers, Verticals/Channels, Targeted New Product Sell-in, Test Markets Results
Customer Relationship Management (CRM)	Formal Customer Satisfaction Surveys, Call Center or Data Collection/Inquiries/Resolutions by Gender. Monitor Online Product Reviews, Discussion Forums, Feedback from Social Media Sites

Women's Leadership Measures and Metrics

YWomen Leadership Measures/Metrics

Area	Measures/Metrics (Develop Gender Baseline, Set Target)
HR Programs and Processes	
Performance Management	Ratings/Ranking Performance by Gender, Disparate Impact Analysis Organizational by Gender, Ratings Calibration Equity by Gender
Compensation	Compensation Equity New Hires, Wage Gap Analysis by Role/Function, Incentive Equity by Gender, Pay Equity by Industry
Learning and Development	Gender/Unconscious Bias Training, Men and Women Working Together for Team Effectiveness, Training for Sales People on Gender Differences, Gender Communications/Influencing Skills
Company Programs	Diversity Advisory Council, Employee Resource Groups, Formal Mentoring, Ombuds/Third Party Resolution
Company Benefits	Formal Flex Time Programs and Usage of (Telecommuting/Compressed Schedule, etc.), Paid Maternity/Adoption Programs (Indexed vs. Industry), Joint Spousal Maternity Leave, On-Site/Subsidized Day Care
Senior Leadership and Other Areas	
Senior Leadership	Divisional Level Plan Development and Reviews, ERG/BRG Sponsorship Engagement, Communication/Initiatives Deployed, Talent Review Process (Diverse Pools, Panels, etc.) adhered to
Board of Directors	Representation, Linkage to Company Mission, Execution/Commitment to Monitor
Procurement	Actual Spend by Women Owned Business, Net New Vendors Engaged/Supported/Created
Staff Functions; Finance/IT, HR	Representation of Agency by Function, Dollars Spent with Women Owned Business/Agencies, Agency Procurement Spend by Vendor
Corporate Reputation/ Communications	
Communication	Formal Communication Strategy and Plan, Reach/Frequency/Effectiveness of Internal and External Written Plan elements, Ranking/Lists, Formal Diversity Report

WHY WOMEN
30-Point Readiness Assessment

1. If you think about the biggest issues that your organization is facing, those challenges that "keep you up at night," how can you better leverage an Integrated Women's Leadership Strategy as a potential solution?

2. As you look at the leadership team around you, does this group think, act, and truly represent the mindset of the majority of your employees and customers?

3. How is your organization moving from a conceptual conversation regarding women to strategies and programs that help to internalize and operationalize a women's leadership strategy for all employees?

4. Does your organization have a framework targeted to women that is designed to grow revenue, improve operating profits, and enhance company reputation?

5. Discuss the concept of Male Gender Blindness in your organization. As you look around the organization, what roles are the women in and how did they get there? One out of two women believes gender bias is still present in companies. What are you doing to combat gender bias in your organization?

6. Male leaders are uncomfortable having conversations regarding gender as they may be seen as insensitive, patronizing, or sexist. What is your organization doing to improve the ability of men to do a better job in providing feedback to women?

7. Regarding revenue, can your organization at all levels articulate your baseline and incremental revenue and profit goals of its women's strategy? What is the current total revenue pie available to you with a focus on women? What percentage are we capturing and what is the revenue/opportunity gap?

8. Regarding talent, what does your organization look like from top to bottom regarding gender, age, and ethnicity? What will your organization look like in five years? How are you capturing the intellectual knowledge of the Boomers who will be retiring shortly?

9. Regarding engagement, does your organization currently have an engagement strategy in place? Are you measuring engagement by gender, race, tenure, and ethnicity? How are we holding managers accountable for increasing engagement?

10. Does your organization, its marketing department, your agency, and your sales force, truly grasp and understand women at a deep level? Does your organization see women as the majority driver of your business or are they classified as a niche?

11. Examine your advertising agency. Do they truly understand and demonstrate expertise in the converging macro-trends of millennials, multicultural employees, and women? What is the composition of your account team including the creative director?

12. Does your sales force know how to sell, prospect, and acquire new customers who are women? Can your sales force clearly articulate the female benefits of your company's products to women?

13. What does your talent pipeline for women look like in the Field? What are the challenges and barriers that you can identify and do you have a plan to address them?

14. As you examine the leadership competency model for your company, how are you developing leaders to evaluate talent that doesn't think, look, and act like they do?

15. Is your leadership prepared to tackle real life issues that impact all talent and are present in organizations today such as The Baby Penalty and new models of work/life responsibilities?

16. Regarding Recruitment, are all of your HR programs and processes both fair and equitable? If you examine job descriptions, are the words used gender neutral? Is your compensation strategy equitable to women?

17. Regarding retention, what are the processes in place to eliminate subjectivity in your performance management system? Are you conducting ongoing diagnostics to insure equitable ratings by gender and race? What elements of diversity training are driving true culture change? Are you leveraging your Business Resource Groups to drive bottom line results?

18. Is your women's development strategy focused on an approach of "fix the women" versus an approach of holding both men and women accountable? Is your leadership engaged in true succession planning and looking at least two levels down in the organization?

19. Does your organization have a sense of urgency regarding its women's leadership strategy and how is it being demonstrated? What elements are contained on your scorecard and at what level of the organization is the scorecard held accountable? How is it being pushed down to the middle management/operating units of your company?

20. Does your organization have hard metrics that it tracks regarding the recruitment, advancement, and retention of women and minorities? Do you publish the numbers to insure organizational transparency? Do the majority of your promotions still go to the largest majority employee population and is this being communicated to minimize backlash? Is compensation tied to a women's/diversity scorecard?

21. Do you and your leadership team understand the significant role that advocates and sponsors play in moving women into the most senior levels of the organization? What is your leadership doing to insure connections and exposure is being given to high potential women?

22. How prepared is your senior leadership team for a public relations nightmare? Do they understand the need for expertise and empathy? Does your website communication pass the connection test of your senior leadership team matching the representation of your diversity pages?

23. Women are using social media to talk about your company and its products and services. What are they saying and what actions are they taking and are these positives or negatives? What are people saying on glassdoor.com about your company?

24. Chances are your company is already doing something in regards to supporting women and communities through its philanthropic and CSR endeavors. Have you ensured that all of your efforts are connected back to your broader Integrated Women's Leadership Strategy?

25. Are you creating a culture that supports your Integrated Women's Leadership Strategy by talking about the business case daily, holding managers accountable, maniacally managing your talent, deepening your cultural competency, and displaying your own commitment? What steps are you taking to insure middle management ownership and engagement?

26. There are four male cultural norms that comprise the "Man Code:" avoid all things feminine, be a winner, show no chinks in the armor, and be a man's man. How do they play themselves out in your organization and how are they inhibiting the growth of women (and male champions)?

27. If you are a father of a daughter, have you made the connection that by not advocating for women today that no one will be advocating for your daughter in the future? What actions are you prepared to take to become an advocate for women within your corporation?

28. Do women in your organization hold other women to higher standards, and have you engaged in a discussion around the challenges and sensitivities that may arise between white women and women of color?

29. Sexual harassment and bullying is a real concern for organizations yet it is rarely talked about or discussed. Is your organization conducting focus groups, feedback sessions, and training sessions to discuss the impact of sexual harassment and bullying and the impact it is having on your organization.

30. Can your organization and its leaders articulate, in financial terms, what the investment is in the company's Integrated Women's Leadership Strategy? If women are truly a priority, how are you staffing against opportunity? Is this a part-time responsibility or do you have full-time dedicated staff as you would with any other business imperative?

Links to Online Articles for "Deepening Your Learning"

Chapter 1: "Can Women Fix Capitalism?" McKinsey & Company (Sep 2014)
http://www.mckinsey.com/insights/leading_in_the_21st_century/can_women_fix_capitalism

Chapter 2: "The Sponsorship Effect: Breaking Through the Last Glass Ceiling," Sylvia Ann Hewlett, Kerrie Peraino, Laura Sherbin, Karen Sumberg
http://www.globalwomen.org.nz/site/globalwomen/files/pdfs/The%20Sponsor%20Effect.pdf

Chapter 3: "2014 Global Human Capital Trends," Deloitte in conjunction with *Forbes* Magazine
http://www.deloitte.com/assets/Dcom-Namibia/GlobalHumanCapitalTrends2014_030714.pdf

Chapter 4: "The Female Economy," Harvard Business Review (Sep 2009)
https://hbr.org/2009/09/the-female-economy

Chapter 5: "Women "Take Care," Men "Take Charge": Stereotyping of U.S. Business Leaders Exposed," Catalyst Research (2005)
http://www.catalyst.org/system/files/Women_Take_Care_Men_Take_Charge_Stereotyping_of_U.S._Business_Leaders_Exposed.pdf

Chapter 6: "Evidence that Gendered Wording in Job Advertisements Exists and Sustains Gender Inequality," Journal of Personality and Social Psychology (2011)
https://faculty.fuqua.duke.edu/~ack23/Publications%20PDF's/gendered%20wording%20JPSP.pdf

Chapter 7: "Global Diversity and Inclusion: Perceptions, Practices, and Attitudes" SHRM (Society for Human Resource Management)
https://www.google.com/?gws_rd=ssl#q=%E2%80%9CGlobal+Diversity+and+Inclusion:+Perceptions%2C+Practices%2C+and+Attitudes%E2%80%9D+SHRM+(Society+for+Human+Resource+Management)

Chapter 8: "Leadership and the Triple Bottom Line," Center for Creative Leadership (2007)
http://www.lesaffaires.com/uploads/references/1190_tripleBottomLine.pdf

Chapter 9: "Engaging Men in Gender Initiative: What Change Agents Need to Know," Catalyst Research (May 2009)
http://www.lesaffaires.com/uploads/references/1190_tripleBottomLine.pdf

Chapter 10: "The Athena Factor: Reversing the Brain Drain in Science, Engineering, and Technology," HBR (June 2008)

http://documents.library.nsf.gov/edocs/HD6060-.A84-2008-PDF-Athena-factor-Reversing-the-brain-drain-in-science,-engineering,-and-technology.pdf

Acknowledgements

There is the journey and there is the book.

The Journey

Though I abhor the use of the word journey when describing an organizational approach to advancing women, it is an entirely appropriate word for this road I have taken over the last thirty-five years in corporate America. First, I could not do this work without the incredible support of my wife and life partner Phyllis.

The next call-out is to some of my oldest friends who have always been there even in the craziest of times: Dave Kirkpatrick, John Byrne, Steve Flaim, Stephen Horgan, Nancy Wollensak-Gilbo, and to my mentor Rick Morgan who is sadly only with me in spirit.

To all the folks, past and present, who I worked with at The Coca-Cola Company. To Mary Nielen who would not let me leave the kick-off meeting of the Coca-Cola Women's Forum without joining a committee. Little did I know how that would end up changing my life. To all the folks at Coca-Cola University who taught me so much every day, especially Karen Hendrix, Tony Brown, Tim Talmadge, Cade Cowan, Jane Finchum, and to all of the alumni and members of the "Facilitator's Network."

To Ed Gadsden and Renae Murphy for teaching me about this "Diversity Thing," and to Lauventria Robinson, Diahann Young, and Kenny Fry for all the great work we did on learning how to create truly integrated diversity leadership strategies.

To the Network of Executive Women (NEW) who have been amazing supporters of my work, especially Joan Toth, Nancy Krawczyk, Kathy Bayert, Stephanie McFee, Eileen Tarjan, Rob Wray, and all of the amazing members both locally and nationally I have had the privilege of working with and for in supporting their mission of advancing women.

I also want to thank the incredible women of NEW Atlanta who are so committed to making our local chapter a success.

To the women and men of the Simmons Business Advisory Board both past and present who I have learned so much from, especially Cathy Minehan, Elisa van Dam, Judy Benjamin, and to Saj-nicole Joni for introducing me to Deborah Merrill-Sands.

I have had the honor of working with and for so many amazing women and men who have supported me and taken me on this journey that it is impossible to thank you all. I do want to give particular thanks to a number of very special people who have provided incredible insights of discovery along the way: Julie Hamilton, Michelle Gloeckler, Susan Gambardella, Kathleen Ciaramello, Cathy Horgan, Alison Kenney Paul, Rohini Anand, Pat Harris, Barbara Annis, Sharon Belto, Genevieve Bos, Kat Cole, Elaine Bowers Coventry, Martha Buffington, Michael Byron, Joe Szombathy, Drew Haynie, Fritzi Woods, Carolyn Jackson, Juli Shook, Rena Holland, Susan Flynn, Amy Whitley, Fawn Germer, Nicole Hutcheson, Melanie Miller, Nadia Bilchik, Daphne Schechter, Lori Addicks, Ashley Berg Jensen, Deb Jeram, Julie Juvera, Barbara Kane, Stuart Kronauge, Amy Levine Samuels, Catherine Lindner, Helene Lollis, Chris Lowe, Mike Mapes, Elisabeth Marchant, Nan McCann, Monica McCoy, Jo Miller, Eric Daly, Erby Foster, Paul F. Murphy, Bea Perez, Marie Quintana, Jacqueline Reynolds, Marilyn Sherman, Sheila Robinson, Sandra Sims-Williams, Sandy Douglas, Rod Tabert, Kathy Caprino, Bonnie Ullman, Ali Hartman, Lori Wilkinson, Ann Nicholas, Jerry Wilson, Oya Yavuz, Gloria Minnick, Hillary Barr, Julie O'Keefe, and Michael Gorshe.

Finally, I would like to acknowledge Tom Peters for his amazing work through the years. Though I have never met you, this work would never have started without your burning passion for change.

The Book

Though these people are listed under "The Book," I could have just as easily listed them under the journey as they all have contributed so much to my life in both areas. There are two people I have to thank as without them, this manuscript would never have seen the light of day. First to Bonnie Daneker for your coaching, mentoring, and support in jump starting this work and for all of the great connections. Second to my Editor John Fayad, for your passion, knowledge, commitment, and gender intelligence in seeing this book through to the end. Thank you both. You are very special friends.

Next, I have literally talked to hundreds of people in researching this book. I want to thank the following people of special significance for their direct contributions of research and stories: Trudy Bourgeois, Bridget Brennan, Carol Evans, John Gerzema, Stacy Blake-Beard, Sandy Sabean, Maria Reitan, Eva Kohn, Kat Gordon, Alice Savic, Barb Poremba, Lynne Siders, Sue Sears, Allison Dukes, Chris Trokey, Melissa Donaldson, Becky Blalock, Tricia Molloy, Jackie Freiberg, Henna Inam, Lynne Homrich, Jolie Weber, Chaly Jo Moyen, Kim Tolmie, Deana Bishop, Rebecca Shambaugh, Connie Glaser, Farnaz Wallace, Michelle Baker, Alyson Daichendt, Lauren de Simone, Mike Grindell, Bobbie O'Hare, Lisa Stoppenbach, Erin Varano, Dawn Kirk, Cathy Sutherland, and Jennifer Wallace.

I also want to thank all of the people who offered their time and support in the final content reviews: Lynn Epstein, Dr. Michelle Byrne, Rani Quirk, Melissa Packman, Candice St. Pierre, Bronwyn Morgan, Mike Patrick, Jeffri Epps, Karyn Hume, Minka Wiggins, Tara Coyt, Janet Smith, Jennifer McKenna, Terri L. Goodrich, Jeffery Halter Jr., Lauren Schmidt-Halter, Heather Kimball, and especially Tricia Brennesholtz for multiple contributions and support in getting this work completed. To Steven Sharp for his layout and design and to Betsy Rhame-Minor for her line editing. Thank you both for your amazing patience and perseverance.

Finally to the amazing Betsy Myers for her encouragement in telling me this book "had to be written," and for agreeing to write my Foreword. Your leadership and commitment to women everywhere continue to motivate me in all of my works. Thanks for being a special friend.

Bibliography

[1] Tom Peters, *Re-Imagine! Business Excellence in a Disruptive Age* (New York: DK Publishing, 2003)

[2] "The Conference Board CEO Challenge® 2014: People and Performance," https://www.conference-board.org/topics/publicationdetail.cfm?publicationid=2681

[3] "Wall Street Questions U.S. Companies' Revenue Growth," http://www.ft.com/intl/cms/s/0/81a008ae-f7f9-11e3-90fa-00144feabdc0.html#axzz3Mj6kO1lM

[4] The Outliers: The Story of Success, (New York, Hachette Book Group, 2008), p. 37

[5] "The Female Economy," *Harvard Business Review,* https://hbr.org/2009/09/the-female-economy

[6] Warren Buffet, "We've Made A 'Terrible Mistake' With Treatment Of Women In America," http://www.businessinsider.com/warren-buffett-on-women-2013-5#ixzz3F0qRuSSS

[7] "2014 State of Women-Owned Businesses Report," http://about.americanexpress.com/news/pr/2014/women-flex-economic-muscle-new-research.aspx

[8] Ibid

[9] "State of the American Workplace," Gallup Research, http://employeeengagement.com/wp-content/uploads/2013/06/Gallup-2013-State-of-the-American-Workplace-Report.pdf

[10] Sylvia Ann Hewlett et al, "The Sponsor Effect: Breaking Through the Last Glass Ceiling," http://www.globalwomen.org.nz/site/globalwomen/files/pdfs/The%20Sponsor%20Effect.pdf

[11] "Women in Senior Management: Setting the Stage for Growth," Grant Thornton International Business Report, 2013, p. 10, http://www.grantthornton.ie/db/Attachments/IBR2013_WiB_report_final.pdf

[12] Sylvia Ann Hewlett et al, "The Sponsor Effect: Breaking Through the Last Glass Ceiling," http://www.globalwomen.org.nz/site/globalwomen/files/pdfs/The%20Sponsor%20Effect.pdf

[13] "Why Men Hate to Give Women Feedback," http://www.forbes.com/sites/work-in-progress/2013/05/01/why-men-hate-to-give-women-feedback/

[14] "Walking on Egg Shells: Fear about talking about differences in the workplace," http://www.diversitycentral.com/tools_and_resources/inclusion/feature_summary_egg_shells.pdf

[15] Muhtar Kent, Chairman & CEO, The Coca-Cola Company, speaking at the World Economic Forum, 2010.

[16] "The Sheconomy: A Guy's Guide to Marketing to Women," http://she-conomy.com/report/marketing-to-women-quick-facts

[17] "How Women Decide, Harvard Business Review, 2013, http://blogs.shu.edu/StillmanLeaders/files/2013/08/HBR-How-Women-Decide.pdf

[18] Beth J. Haslett, Florence L. Geis, Mae R. Carter, *The Organizational Woman*, (Santa Barbara: Praeger Publishing 1992), p 2

[19] "The Rise of Women: Seven Charts Showing Women's Rapid Gains in Educational Achievement," http://www.russellsage.org/blog/rise-women-seven-charts-showing-womens-rapid-gains-educational-achievement

[20] "A Guide to Metro Atlanta's Education Leaders," http://www.bizjournals.com/atlanta/print-edition/2012/05/11/a-guide-to-metro-atlantas-education.html?page=all

21 "Ready or Not, First Baby Boomers Turn 65 This Year,"
http://money.usnews.com/money/blogs/on-
retirement/2012/03/23/the-baby-boomer-number-game

22 "State of the American Workplace: Employee Engagement Insights
for U.S. Business Leaders,"
http://www.michaeljbeck.com/documents/State%20of%20the%20Am
erican%20Workplace%20Report%202013.pdf

23 Bridget Brennan, *Why She Buys: The New Strategy for Reaching the World's
Most Powerful Consumers* (New York: Crown Publishing, 2011) p.5.

24 "The Sheconomy: A Guy's Guide to Marketing to Women,"
http://she-conomy.com/report/marketing-to-women-quick-facts

25 Fara Warner, *Power of the Purse: How Smart Businesses Are Adapting to the
World's Most Important Consumer—Women* (New Jersey: FT Press, 2005) p.
184

26 "The Sheconomy: A Guy's Guide to Marketing to Women,"
http://she-conomy.com/report/marketing-to-women-quick-facts

27 Interview with Sandy Sabean, Founder & Chief Creative Officer,
Womankind, September 2014

28 "The Female Economy," *Harvard Business Review* (September 2009)
https://hbr.org/2009/09/the-female-economy

29 Bridget Brennan, "The Real Reason Women Shop More than Men,"
Forbes (March 2013)
http://www.forbes.com/sites/bridgetbrennan/2013/03/06/the-real-
reason-women-shop-more-than-men/

30 Farnaz Wallace, *The New World Marketplace, how Women, Youth and
Multiculturalism are Shaping Our Future* (Oklahoma: Tate Publishing, 2012)
Kindle edition

31 Interview with Sandy Sabean, Chief Creative Officer, Womankind,
September 2014

[32] "Nike opens store just for women, believes women's business will outpace men's by 2017," *BizWomen Business Journals* (November 2014) http://www.bizjournals.com/bizwomen/news/latest-news/2014/11/nike-opens-store-just-for-women-believes-womens.html?page=all

[33] "Stats on Women," Jamie Dunham, Brand Wise, http://jamiedunham.com/stats-on-women/

[34] Marti Barletta, *PrimeTime Women: How to Win the Hearts, Minds, and Business of Boomer Big Spenders* (New York, Kaplan Publishing, 2007) p. 1

[35] "Women as investors: Opportunities for advisors," https://advisors.vanguard.com/VGApp/iip/site/advisor/researchcommentary/article/IWE_InvComWomenInvestorsOp

[36] "Marketing to Women: Quick Facts," http://she-conomy.com/facts-on-women

[37] "Women-Drivers.com," http://women-drivers.com/mid-year-report-top-brands-rated-by-women-when-purchasing/

[38] Conversations M2W Conference (April 2014)

[39] Ibid

[40] "The 3% Conference," Championing Creative Female Talent + Leadership, http://www.3percentconf.com/blog

[41] Ibid

[42] "Walmart to enhance spending goals as part of its Global Women's Economic Empowerment program" http://diversityandcommerce.biz/front-page-walmart-to-enhance-spending-goals-as-part-of-its-global-women-p2546-109.htm

[43] "TAB Energy Drink," *http://www.bevnet.com/reviews/tab_energy/*

[44] "TAB Energy," *http://www.caffeineinformer.com/caffeine-content/tab-energy*

[45] Jim Collins, *Good to Great* (New York: HarperBusiness, 2001) p. 11

46 "Women CEOs of the Fortune 1000,"
http://www.catalyst.org/knowledge/women-ceos-fortune-1000

47 Ibid

48 "Moving Mind-Sets on Gender Diversity: McKinsey Global Survey results,"
http://www.mckinsey.com/insights/organization/moving_mind-sets_on_gender_diversity_mckinsey_global_survey_results

49 "Women Take Care Men Take Charge,"
http://www.apa.org/pubs/journals/features/mgr-12-1-25.pdf p.13

50 Sylvia Ann Hewlett et al, "The Sponsor Effect: Breaking Through the Last Glass Ceiling,"
http://www.globalwomen.org.nz/site/globalwomen/files/pdfs/The%20Sponsor%20Effect.pdf p. 8

51 "Differences in How Men and Women Think Are Hard-Wired,"
http://online.wsj.com/news/articles/SB10001424052702304744304579248151866594232

52 "Brain Connectivity Study Reveals Striking Differences Between Men and Women,"
http://www.uphs.upenn.edu/news/News_Releases/2013/12/verma/

53 "Women 'Take Care', Men 'Take Charge': Stereotyping of U.S. Business Leadership Exposed,"
http://www.catalyst.org/system/files/Women_Take_Care_Men_Take_Charge_Stereotyping_of_U.S._Business_Leaders_Exposed.pdf

54 "The Double-Bind Dilemma for Women in Leadership: Damned if You Do, Doomed if You Don't,"
http://www.catalyst.org/knowledge/double-bind-dilemma-women-leadership-damned-if-you-do-doomed-if-you-dont-0

55 "Women Are Still Doing Most of the Housework,"
http://time.com/2895235/men-housework-women/#2895235/men-housework-women/

56 "Modern Parenthood: Roles of Moms and Dads Converge as They Balance Work and Family,"
http://www.pewsocialtrends.org/2013/03/14/modern-parenthood-roles-of-moms-and-dads-converge-as-they-balance-work-and-family/

57 Interview with Carol Evans, CEO and President of *Working Mother* Magazine (September 2014, February 2015)

58 "U.S. Women on the Rise as Family Breadwinners," *New York Times* (May 2013),
http://www.nytimes.com/2013/05/30/business/economy/women-as-family-breadwinner-on-the-rise-study-says.html?_r=0

59 Cheryl Conner, "The 10 Paradoxical Commandments of Business,"
http://www.forbes.com/sites/cherylsnappconner/2012/08/28/the-10-paradoxical-commandments-of-business-for-entrepreneurs/

60 "Gale Directory of Company Histories: The Coca-Cola Company,"
http://www.answers.com/topic/the-coca-cola-company

61 Gaucher, D., Friesen, J., and Kay, A. C., "Evidence That Gendered Wording in Job Advertisements Exists and Sustains Gender Inequality," *Journal of Personality and Social Psychology,* (2011)
https://faculty.fuqua.duke.edu/~ack23/Publications%20PDFs/gendered%20wording%20JPSP.pdf p. 2

62 "The Simple Truth about the Gender Pay Gap,"
http://www.aauw.org/files/2013/03/The-Simple-Truth-Fall-2013.pdf

63 Ibid

64 http://www.catalyst.org/knowledge/womens-earnings-and-income

65 Linda Babcock and Sara Laschever, *Women Don't Ask: The High Cost of Avoiding Negotiation—And Positive Strategies for Change* (New Jersey: Princeton University Press, 2003) p.1

66 Rebecca Shambaugh, *It's Not a Glass Ceiling it's a Sticky Floor:* Free Yourself From the Hidden Behaviors Sabotaging Your Career Success (New York, McGraw-Hill, 2007) p. 22

67 "Quotations from Chairman Powell: A Leadership Primer,"
http://govleaders.org/powell.htm

[68] "Measurement Myopia," Drucker Institute,
http://www.druckerinstitute.com/2013/07/measurement-myopia/

[69] "Diversity Metrics Determine the Four Stages of Diversity Management," http://www.diversityinc.com/diversity-metrics/diversity-metrics-determine-the-four-stages-of-diversity-management/

[70] "Living Our Commitment: Diversity, Inclusion, Engagement," Walgreens 2013 Diversity & Inclusion Report,
www.walgreens.com/topic/sr/sr_diversity_inclusion_report.jsp

[71] "Global Diversity and Inclusion," Society for Human Resource Management,
http://graphics.eiu.com/upload/eb/DiversityandInclusion.pdf, p. 12

[72] Ibid

[73] "The 2014 Diversity Inc. Top 50 Companies for Diversity,"
http://www.diversityinc.com/about-the-diversityinc-top-50/

[74] "Diversity-Management Case Studies Reveal Why Companies Rise and Fall in the Diversity Inc. Top 50"
http://www.diversityinc.com/diversity-management/why-companies-rise-and-fall/

[75] "Top Five Ways CEO Show Commitment to Diversity,"
http://www.diversitybestpractices.com/events/top-five-ways-ceos-show-commitment-diversity?pnid=7876

[76] "The Sponsor Effect: Breaking Through the Last Glass Ceiling," Sylvia Ann Hewlett, Kerrie Peraino, Laura Sherbin, and Karen Sumberg, Center for Work-Life Policy
http://www.globalwomen.org.nz/site/globalwomen/files/pdfs/The%20Sponsor%20Effect.pdf

[77] "The Hidden Brain Drain: Off-Ramps and On-Ramps in Women's Careers," https://hbr.org/product/hidden-brain-drain-off-ramps-and-on-ramps-in-women-s-careers/9491-PDF-ENG

[78] Daniel Diermeier, *Reputation Rules* book interview,
http://eandt.theiet.org/magazine/2011/09/book-interview.cfm

[79] "Target Data Breach Has Lasting Effects," http://nypost.com/2014/01/10/target-data-breach-fallout-could-have-lasting-effects/

[80] "Four Perspectives on Re-establishing Trust," Daniel Deirmeier (May 2012) https://reprules.wordpress.com/2012/05/18/four-perspectives-on-re-establishing-trust/

[81] Daniel Diermeier, *Reputation Rules: Strategies for Building Your Company's Most Valuable Asset*, (New York, McGraw-Hill, 2011) p. 4

[82] Ibid, p. 22

[83] "Living Our Values: Marathon Oil 2013 Corporate Social Responsibility report," http://www.marathonoil.com/Social_Responsibility/Reporting/2013_CSR_Report/Workplace/Recruiting_Training_and_Development/

[84] http://www.ratemyprofessors.com/

[85] "The Triple Win: the Impact of Greening your Organization," http://www.eco-coach.com/blog/2009/04/17/the-triple-win-the-impact-of-greening-your-organization/

[86] Ibid

[87] Net Impact Talent Report: "What Workers Want in 2012," https://netimpact.org/sites/default/files/documents/what-workers-want-2012.pdf

[88] Pew Research Internet Project: "Social Networking Project," (January 2014) http://www.pewinternet.org/fact-sheets/social-networking-fact-sheet/

[89] "She's Connected," Women's Marketing Inc., and SheSpeaks, (June 2012) http://www.womensmarketing.com/blog/2012/06/shes-connected-presented-by-womens-marketing-inc-and-shespeaks/

[90] Ibid

[91] Bonnie Ulman and Sal Kibler, *Hustle, Marketing to Women in the Post-Recession World* (New York: Paramount Market Publishing, Inc., 2013)

[92] Barbara Annis & Associates, Gender Surveys 2005 to 2012

[93] "How Many Blogs Are On the Internet?"
http://www.wpvirtuoso.com/how-many-blogs-are-on-the-internet

[94] "Bob Moritz: Helping to Bring Men to the Table," *Forbes* (January 2014) http://www.forbes.com/sites/bonniemarcus/2014/01/28/bob-moritz-helping-to-bring-men-to-the-table/

[95] http://www.merriam-webster.com/medical/maniacal

[96] "What It's Like Being a Middle Manager Today," *Wall Street Journal* (August 2013)
http://online.wsj.com/news/articles/SB10001424127887323420604578650074170664066

[97] "Hold The Applause: Gaining Middle Management Buy-in to The Success of Your Diversity Initiative,"
http://www.multiculturaladvantage.com/recruit/diversity/Hold-The-Applause.asp

[98] "Engaging Men in Gender Initiatives: What Change Agents Need To Know," http://www.catalyst.org/knowledge/engaging-men-gender-initiatives-what-change-agents-need-know p. 9

[99] Madeline Albright keynote speech at *Celebrating Inspiration* luncheon with the WNBA's All-Decade Team, 2006
http://www.networkworld.com/article/2164853/infrastructure-management/madeleine-albright---there-s-a-special-place-in-hell-reserved-for-women-wh.html

[100] "Top 5 Things You Never Discuss at Work,"
http://excelle.monster.com/benefits/articles/1538-top-5-things-you-never-discuss-at-work

[101] "Women Penalized for Promoting Women, Study Finds," Wall Street Journal (July 2014) http://blogs.wsj.com/atwork/2014/07/21/women-penalized-for-promoting-women-study-finds/

[102] "Tapestry: Leveraging the Rich Diversity of Women in Retail and Consumer Goods," Network of Executive Women, (October 2014)
http://www.newonline.org/?page=tapestry

[103] November 4, 2014 interview with Trudy Bourgeois, CEO of Center Workforce Excellence

[104] November 4, 2014 interview with Stacy Blake-Beard, Professor of Management at the Simmons College, School of Management

[105] "Harassment at work: 52% of women report bullying," CNBC, (April 2014) http://www.cnbc.com/id/101547838

[106] "New Study Reports Sexual Harassment, Assault May be Dissuading Women from Careers in Science," (July 2014) http://www.truth-out.org/news/item/25212-new-study-reports-sexual-harassment-assault-may-be-dissuading-women-from-careers-in-science

[107] "The Athena Factor: Reversing the Brain Drain in Science, Engineering, and Technology," *Harvard Business Review* (June 2008) http://documents.library.nsf.gov/edocs/HD6060-.A84-2008-PDF-Athena-factor-Reversing-the-brain-drain-in-science,-engineering,-and-technology.pdf

[108] Sarah Lewis, *The Rise: Creativity, the Gift of Failure, and the Search for Mastery*, (New York: Simon & Schuster, 2014) p. 8

[109] "Professional Women Choosing Flexibility Over Higher Pay," U.S. News, 2011 http://money.usnews.com/money/blogs/outside-voices-careers/2011/11/17/professional-women-choosing-flexibility-over-higher-pay

[110] Ibid

[111] "A Blueprint for Change," *Wall Street Journal*, (April 2011) http://www.wsj.com/articles/SB10001424052748704415104576250900113069980

[112] "Bob Moritz: Helping to Bring Men to the Table," *Forbes* (January 2014), http://www.forbes.com/sites/bonniemarcus/2014/01/28/bob-moritz-helping-to-bring-men-to-the-table/

[113] Jeanne C. Meister, Karie Willyerd, "The 2020 Workplace: How Innovative Companies Attract, Develop, and Keep Tomorrow's Employees Today," (New York: Harperbusiness, 2010) p. 13

114 John Gerzema, *The Athena Doctrine: How Women (and the Men Who Think Like Them) Will Rule the Future*, (San Francisco, Jossey-Bass, 2013) p. 261

115 "The Top 25 Best Countries To Be A Woman," Huffington Post (March, 2014) http://www.huffingtonpost.com/2014/03/11/best-countries-for-women_n_4549918.html

116 "Massachusetts Companies Join Groundbreaking Effort to Close the Gender Gap at Work," Bentley University Center for Women and Business," (October 2014) http://www.bentley.edu/centers/sites/www.bentley.edu.centers/files/2014/10/10/Gov%20Corp%20Challenge%20news%20release%20-%20FINAL.pdf

117 "Companies With More Women Board Directors Experience Higher Financial Performance, According to Latest Catalyst Bottom Line Report," (October 2007) http://www.catalyst.org/media/companies-more-women-board-directors-experience-higher-financial-performance-according-latest

118 Interview with Maria Reitan, November 4, 2014.

119 "Women Moving Millions," http://www.womenmovingmillions.org/

120 "Sallie Krawcheck Opens an Index Fund Focused on Women, *New York Times,* (June 2014), http://dealbook.nytimes.com/2014/06/04/sallie-krawcheck-opens-an-index-fund-focused-on-women/

121 Interview with Carol Evans, CEO and President of *Working Mother* Magazine (September 2014)

122 Sheryl Sandberg, *Lean-In, Women, Work and the Will to Lead, (*New York, Random House, 2013) p. 8

123 Katty Kay & Claire Shipman, *The Confidence Code, The Science and Art of Self-Assurance-What Women Should Know,* (New York, HarperCollins Publishers, 2014) p. 12

124 "Why Women Still Can't Have It All," *The Atlantic* Magazine (July 2007), http://www.theatlantic.com/magazine/archive/2012/07/why-women-still-cant-have-it-all/309020/

Index

N

O

P

T

U

W

Y

Z

YWomen

Jeffery Tobias Halter is a "Y" Chromosome that "Gets Women."

About Jeffery

Jeffery is a consultant, gender strategist, and the President of YWomen. YWomen is a strategic consulting company focused on helping men (i.e., Y Chromosomes) and women to understand and unleash the power of women in organizations.

Jeffery is a sought-after speaker for television and radio appearances, keynotes, workshops or to moderate a panel. Topics include: *Why Women The Leadership Imperative*, (the keynote based on this book), *Executive Success: What Men Aren't Telling Women; The EVOLVED Leader: Men and Women Working Together for Team Success;* and *Selling to Men, Selling to Women.* Speaking engagements and consultations can be tailored and customized to address your specific goals and objectives. To learn more about Jeffery and his work go to: www.ywomen.biz. You may also reach out to him directly at: jthalter@ywomen.biz.

The Father of Daughter Initiative

Fathers of Daughters have a special responsibility to become advocates for women in the workplace. The Fathers of Daughters Initiative is an easy-to-do opt-in program for men to demonstrate their commitment to advancing women. The Father of Daughter Initiative on the following page may be cut out and placed on your desk. Read it, commit to do at least one thing on the list, and sign it. You may also download The Fathers of Daughters Initiative at www.ywomen.biz. This simple action immediately demonstrates that you are advocating for women because you understand the responsibility of a Father of a Daughter.

The Father of Daughter Challenge

As the father of a daughter, I will LISTEN, LEARN, LEAD and have the WILL to advocate for the equitable treatment of women in the workplace.

I am making this commitment in support of my daughter(s):

_____

As the Father of a Daughter, I pledge to do one or more of the following…

1. Seek to Understand – Find a female co-worker, someone I can have an honest conversation with, and listen to the experiences she is having as a woman in my company.

2. Mentor and Sponsor – Mentor a female co-worker. If applicable, become a sponsor for a woman.

3. Create a Business Case – Write a brief business case for my department or area of responsibility for women regarding revenue, talent or engagement and discuss it with my team once a month during the coming year.

4. Set An Example to Correct Bias – Act to correct micro bias; from simple things like always having a woman take notes, to women being talked over in meetings or other actions that serve to exclude women from conversations and activities.

5. Embrace Workplace Flexibility – Support and demonstrate workplace flexibility for all employees, so that women don't feel they are being singled out for special treatment.

6. Offer Encouragement – I will encourage women to take more risks, volunteer for stretch projects, and discuss and support their developmental needs.

7. Support Gender Pay Equity – Deepen my understanding of my company's HR practices, specifically gender pay equity issues and work to correct issues I discover.

8. Encourage Qualified Women to Apply – Urge qualified women to interview for positions when they become available, and if I cannot find a qualified one, commit to developing a woman for the next opening.

9. Engage other Men – Engage other fathers of daughters in the discussion of advancing women.

10. Be a Champion – Demonstrate my commitment by joining/attending a women's resource group or event. Be a visible advocate.

Name:_____ Date:_____